# CONTENTS

# ABOUT THE AUTHORS

**James Barber** is a member of the Centre of International Studies at Cambridge University. He was formerly Master of Hatfield College and Professor of Politics at Durham University. His book *South Africa in the Twentieth Century* will be published by Blackwell's in 1999.

**Jesmond Blumenfeld** is associate senior lecturer in economics at Brunel University, and associate tutor in economics at the Department of Continuing Education at the University of Oxford. He is also editor of the quarterly Bulletin of the Centre for Economic Policy Research (CEPR) in London, joint Region Head for Africa at Oxford Analytica, and a member of the editorial board of *African Affairs*. He has been Associate Research Fellow on Southern Africa at the Royal Institute of International Affairs and was the founding convenor of the current Chatham House Study Group on Southern Africa. He has written widely on the political economy of South and southern Africa and on South Africa's international economic relations.

**Heather Deegan** is head of International Studies at Middlesex University, London and a Research Fellow of the Africa Institute of South Africa, Pretoria. She has been researching the process of democratic change in South Africa since 1994, during which time she was a visiting lecturer at the University of Witwatersrand. Her latest book, *South Africa Reborn: Building a new Democracy* (UCL Press/Routledge), was published in 1998.

**Graham Evans** is Senior Lecturer in International Relations at the University of Wales, Swansea. He has held a number of senior visiting posts at universities and research institutes in South and southern Africa, and has published widely on foreign policy and international affairs. He has also worked for the United Nations and the Organization for Security and Cooperation in Europe as electoral supervisor in South Africa, Mozambique and Bosnia-Hercegovina. His latest publication is *The Penguin Dictionary of International Relations* (1998).

**Merle Lipton** is Senior Research Fellow at the School of African and Asian Studies at Sussex University. She is the author of *Capitalism & Apartheid: South Africa, 1910–86* (Wildwood Press, UK, 1986); 'The Challenge of Sanctions' (Centre for the Study of the South African Economy & Finance at the LSE, 1991); co-editor with Charles Simkins of *State & Market in Post-apartheid South Africa* (Witwatersrand University Press, 1993), and co-editor with Michael Lipton, Mike de Klerk and Frank Ellis of *Land, Labour and Livelihoods in Rural South Africa* (Indicator Press, 1996).

**James Mayall** is Sir Patrick Sheehy Professor of International Relations and Director of the Centre of International Studies at the University of Cambridge. A former member of the Council of Chatham House, he is author of *Nationalism and International Society* (Cambridge University Press, 1990), and editor of and contributor to *The New Interventionism: UN Experience in Cambodia, Former Yugoslavia and Somalia* (Cambridge University Press, 1996).

**Greg Mills** is the National Director of the South African Institute of International Affairs, Johannesburg. He has published widely in the field of southern African politics.

**Sir Patrick Moberly** is a former diplomat and was Ambassador to South Africa, 1984–7. He has been Chairman of the Southern Africa Study Group at Chatham House since 1989.

**Khehla Shubane** is a Research Officer at the Centre for Policy Studies, Johannesburg, and an authority on South African politics.

**David Simon** is Reader in Development Geography and Director of the Centre for Developing Areas Research (CEDAR), Department of Geography, Royal Holloway, University of London. He has published widely on many aspects of development, with particular reference to sub-Saharan Africa, and is also a Namibian and South African specialist. His latest books are *South Africa in Southern Africa: Reconfiguring the Region* (ed. James Currey/David Philip; Ohio UP, 1998) and *Development as Theory and Practice: Current Perspectives on Development and Development Co-operation* (co-editor; Longman, 1999).

**J. E. Spence** was Director of Studies at the Royal Institute of International Affairs (1991–7) and is an Associate Fellow of the Institute. He is currently Visiting Lecturer at King's College, London and Academic Advisor at the Royal College of Defence Studies, London.

**Stanley Uys** was educated at the University of Cape Town and has an honorary doctorate in law from the University of Calgary, Canada. He was formerly Political Editor of the *Johannesburg Sunday Times* and South African correspondent of the *Guardian, Observer,* and *New Statesman* (1960–76). He was London editor for *Times Media* (1977–86). He has contributed to various journals and published three books on South Africa and Namibia.

**David Welsh** was born in Cape Town and taught in the Department of Political Studies at the University of Cape Town until his retirement in 1997; he is now Emeritus Professor of Political Studies. He has written extensively about South African politics and the politics of divided societies.

# ABBREVIATIONS AND ACRONYMS

ACDP      African Christian Democratic Party
ACRI      African Crisis Response Initiative
ANC      African National Congress
AZAPO      Azanian People's Organization
CBO      Community-based organization
COSATU      Congress of South African Trade Unions
DFA      Department of Foreign Affairs
DP      Democratic Party
ECOWAS      Economic Community of West African States
FDI      Foreign direct investment
FF      Freedom Front
GEAR      Growth, Employment and Redistribution programme
GDP      Gross domestic product
GNU      Government of National Unity
IDASA      Institute for Democracy in South Africa
IFP      Inkatha Freedom Party
IMF      International Monetary Fund
IOR      Indian Ocean Rim–Association for Regional Cooperation
KZN      KwaZulu Natal
MDM      Mass Democratic Movement
NAM      Non-Aligned Movement
NCOP      National Council of Provinces
NEC      National Executive Committee
NEDLAC      National Economic Development and Labour Council
NGO      Non-governmental organization
(N)NP      (New) National Party
OAU      Organization of African Unity
PAC      Pan Africanist Congress
RDP      Reconstruction and Development Programme
SACP      South African Communist Party
SADC      Southern African Development Community
SADF      South African Defence Force
SAIRR      South African Institute of Race Relations
SANCO      South African National Civic Organization
SANDF      South African National Defence Force
TRC      Truth and Reconciliation Commission
UDF      United Democratic Front
UDM      United Democratic Movement

# FOREWORD

South Africa is never far these days from the attention of politicians, business people, journalists and others around the world. The famous landmark elections in 1994, vivid evidence in themselves of the shift in political power after apartheid, are to be followed by another round of elections this year, when the eyes of many nations will again be on South Africa.

Nowhere will the future course of events be watched more closely than in Britain, seen through the prism of its long-standing connections with South Africa. The Mandela era is nearing its end. What should we expect of its successor?

This publication brings together the views of a number of experienced observers, both British and South African, as they assess the complex mixture of political, economic and international issues at stake.

The picture that emerges is of the sometimes uneven achievements of the past five years, backed by an underlying resilience in South Africa's institutions and creativity, which have nevertheless to be balanced against an array of challenges facing the new government. While admitting to some uncertainty about the way ahead, contributors leave us with the impression that South Africa's transformation may continue to be seen as an overall success story for this often troubled continent.

The role of the Southern Africa Study Group deserves a further word from me, as its chairman. Long established as a forum for discussion of southern African affairs at Chatham House, the Study Group is now raising its profile in various ways, including the commissioning of more published material. I believe the present volume is an excellent move in that direction.

Over many years there have of course been a number of well-received Chatham House publications about South Africa, sometimes drawing upon views and ideas exchanged within the Study Group. But it is a relatively new departure for the Southern Africa Study Group as such to commission and sponsor its own substantial piece of work, under the overall impetus of Chatham House.

Our thanks go not only to Professor Spence for his drive and enthusiasm as editor, and to his team of authors, but also to the Le Poer Power Trust whose funding of the research involved has enabled us to bring this initiative to life. A special word of thanks, too to George Joffé, Margaret May and Susan Walker, each of whom provided much practical support as the project neared completion.

*April 1999*                                                                 Sir Patrick Moberly
Chairman, Chatham House Southern Africa Study Group

# 1 INTRODUCTION

## J. E. Spence*

South Africa's elections on 2 June 1999 mark the end of a five-year transition dominated by the towering personality of its president, Nelson Mandela. Given the certain victory of the African National Congress (ANC) in the election and the accession of Thabo Mbeki as Mandela's successor, domestic and international attention will focus heavily on the new president's political style, his capacity to keep his nerve in difficult economic circumstances and his strategy of 'transformation'.

This paper has been designed to provide a commentary on the background to the election and – in particular – the government's record over the last five years. It also attempts some informed speculation on the impact of a Mbeki-led administration on the structure and process of South African politics as the country enters the new millennium; the performance of the economy; the prospects for social transformation following the report of the Truth and Reconciliation Commission (TRC); and the future direction of foreign policy. These themes, *inter alia*, are discussed in detail by the various contributors to this study. This introduction highlights some of the more pressing concerns that will preoccupy the new government.

As for the election itself, the ANC – and Mbeki in particular as president in waiting – is campaigning on its achievements and aspirations for the future, stressing its commitment to accelerate the delivery of social goods – such as housing, education, health-care provision – to the deprived black majority. Mbeki too will emphasize his personal commitment to the Growth, Employment and Redistribution programme (GEAR) as the vital instrument for rejuvenating an economy whose performance has not matched the expectations of the founding fathers of the new South Africa, its overseas well-wishers and potential business partners. In particular, the overwhelming priority of job creation is a key issue in electoral debate, although there is disagreement about the best means of reducing unemployment, estimated at three million (i.e. some 30 per cent of the country's adult population). Despite some reference to foreign policy – to 'Building a Better Africa and a Better World', as Mbeki stressed in the election manifesto published in late March 1999, for the great bulk of the electorate,

* The editor is grateful to Sir Patrick Moberly, Chairman of the Chatham House Southern Africa Study Group, for his kind assistance and wise counsel in the preparation of this paper.

1

this will be a relatively minor issue in the campaign with the primary emphasis placed on social and economic issues and the critical importance of reducing crime.

A persistent theme in the election is the likelihood or otherwise of the ANC securing a two-thirds majority of seats in the National Assembly. This outcome would enable a new government to change the constitution – a matter of concern to opposition parties which rightly place their faith in existing safeguards against abuse of power and the emergence of a *de facto* one-party state. Yet there is no evidence that constitutional change is on the ANC's agenda; rather, it seeks a massive endorsement of its five-year record in office, strengthened legitimacy and a genuinely popular mandate for a second term. Indeed, even if the ANC were to secure a two-thirds majority, it is hard to see what advantage a newly empowered government would gain from making controversial amendments to a constitution which has served well enough till now.

## The Mandela legacy: the political context

Mbeki inherits a stable political system with no significant threat to its continued viability. Populist revolt and violent white right-wing reaction are improbable. Isolated acts of political violence during the election may occur, especially in the Western Cape where a variety of fundamentalist Muslim groups have resorted to terrorism against community leaders and ANC personnel, or, alternatively, have taken the law into their own hands against drug dealers and criminals. In KwaZulu-Natal violence has declined dramatically and both the ANC and the Inkatha Freedom Party (IFP) have made serious efforts to reach political accommodation. But if the state remains secure in its legitimacy and capacity to deter and defend against widespread insurrection, its leadership, both present and future, have to deal with a level of criminal violence that has reached alarming proportions since the transition to democracy. Violent crime will certainly figure in the election and the opposition parties will emphasize its deleterious impact on both domestic and foreign perceptions of South Africa's long-term attractiveness as an emerging market for investors, tourism (potentially a major growth industry) and those who see the country as an exception to the malaise that afflicts so many of its counterparts elsewhere. Although there has been some decline in the incidence of violent crime and a variety of initiatives are under way to reduce it still further, much will depend on radical reform of the police service, its capacity for recruitment, better training methods and more efficient use of resources. And this strategy can only reap maximum benefit over the longer term.

For liberal critics both at home and abroad, the absence of a viable and united parliamentary opposition is a cardinal weakness in South Africa's political system. The current crop of parties are clearly too disparate and lacking in electoral support to pose as an alternative government; nor can they adopt the alternative root and branch posture – 'opposition for opposition's sake' – since all, to a varying degree, support the GEAR strategy and the government's commitment to fiscal prudence, and acknowledge that global economic imperatives leave scant room for manoeuvre. Similarly, their leaders do not dispute the crucial importance of delivering social benefits to the black majority.

Thus there is no major ideological divide between government and opposition and party debate is (and will remain) largely about the pace of policy implementation and the means deemed appropriate for its achievement. However, as our analysis makes clear, the ANC, caught between its origins as a liberation movement and what is required of an orthodox and mature party of government, is at times ambivalent about the notion of a loyal opposition charged with responsibility for constructive criticism (however remote its capacity to do so may seem at present) and even 'throwing the rascals out'. For some in the movement, Mbeki included, opposition criticism is profoundly irritating and perceived as destructive sniping on the fringes of a 'transforming' South Africa.

Understandably, critics have focused on the danger of 'democratic centralism' as the central thrust of a Mbeki regime. Aiming to be inclusive (the legacy of its liberation mode), the ANC will – it is argued – pay less and less attention to its opposition counterparts, becoming complacent, even arrogant, and less constrained by the political virtues of accountability, responsibility and transparency in decision-making. Indeed, as some theorists have argued, these virtues only flourish in a climate where opposition is legal, well organized and articulate in their defence, reinforcing their application as a litmus test of a government's behaviour.

Yet the question remains: is South Africa an exception to the well-trodden path leading to one-party dictatorship so familiar elsewhere on the continent during the early years of independence from colonial rule? Several important qualifications to this bleak thesis deserve consideration:

- If parliamentary opposition is weak – with the notable exception of the Democratic Party (DP) under the effective leadership of Tony Leon – there are nonetheless important sources of informal opposition in the shape of a critical press, a multitude of non-governmental organizations (NGOs), a variety of independent research institutions and a sophisticated intellectual class well versed in argument and debate.
- Traditionally, South Africa has had the advantage of a vigorous civil society, in large part the creation of individuals and organizations during the apartheid years. As argument in this paper makes clear, difficulties have arisen since 1994 with respect to NGOs' relations with the state, but their continuing strength and capacity for vociferous dissent should not be underestimated.

- The members of the business community constitute a powerful lobby whose voice finds expression – together with that of the trade union movement – in the National Economic Development and Labour Council (NEDLAC). Indeed the pressures of a global market economy dictate a symbiotic relationship between the government and the private sector in which neither can dominate to the detriment of the other.
- The role of parliamentary committees, despite the constraints upon their capacity to provide full accountability, constitutes a brake of sorts on executive action and may in time develop a more significant and critical role – especially if the current informal system of constituency representation evolves into a more substantial source of local pressure.

## Economic and social perspectives

Here again performance to date has been mixed: the government has shown admirable persistence in sticking to the goals of the GEAR programme, although the record of implementation has been uneven. Mbeki has no alternative but to maintain the government's commitment despite periodic bursts of opposition from the ANC's alliance partners – the South African Communist Party (SACP) and the Congress of South African Trade Unions (COSATU). But like its counterparts elsewhere on the continent, the government is caught in an all too familiar dilemma: the short-term pain involved in restructuring the economy in line with the IMF/World Bank view on what has to be done by way of liberalization, deregulation and privatization threatens to overwhelm whatever social benefits may accrue over the long term. Thus Mbeki will have to strike a balance between the constraints of a global marketplace, and pressure from within his party as well as the wider domestic constituency to modify the programme in favour of quicker returns in the economic and social fields. Tipping the scales too far in either direction will involve considerable risks, which are examined in detail in this paper. In particular, the consequences of persisting with an inflexible labour policy as outlined in recent legislation are discussed, and it is worth noting in passing that Mbeki appears willing to consider its revision.

The likely thrust of future policy must also take account of an economy currently in recession with growth rates of 0.2 per cent in 1998 and a prediction of 1–1.5 per cent for 1999. There is no sign of a significant fall in the high interest rates, although inflation remains in single figures, varying in recent months from 8.5 to 6.5 per cent. Despite the rand's dramatic depreciation during 1998/9 exports have fallen, as have agricultural and mining production. Ultimately, Mbeki will have to force the pace of deregulation and privatization if the economy is to grow to match an annual 2.5 per cent increase in population and attract the foreign direct investment which has so far failed to materialize on any significant scale.

4

As for social provision, the Mandela government has a respectable record with respect to clean water and electrification in black communities. But much remains to be done to correct profound deficiencies in black education, skills training and health provision. Education is critical if employment prospects are to improve and compensate for the loss of white skills via emigration prompted by the impact of affirmative action on employment prospects and crime rates. The latest figures are revealing: some 9,410 people – of whom 1,928 were professionals – left South Africa in 1997.[1] Recent surveys indicate that 75 per cent of newly qualified chartered accountants seek work abroad, while a 1997 report claimed that 13 per cent of executives had left the country. Between 1994 and 1996 2,866 professionals left the country.[2]

## Foreign policy

Mbeki is clearly aware that his conduct of foreign policy will lack his predecessor's personal impact on the country's standing in the international community. But personality, reputation and the memory of a remarkable transition to democracy are declining assets as South Africa becomes 'just another country', competing as best it can with other emerging markets for a place on the agendas of multinational companies and governments alike. How to reconcile the promotion of an African Renaissance (Mbeki's personal brain-child) with domestic imperatives demanding a perpetual search for new markets and sources of investment will be a central preoccupation of the new government. As our analysis indicates, relations with the West will remain important despite an emerging pattern of conflict and cooperation where interests coincide. Equally, there is a desire to avoid the stigma of being an outpost of Western influence, cut off from a constructive role in the Third World. These issues are explored in some depth, together with the incentives and constraints attendant upon the country's hegemonic position in the southern African region and the pressure on the government from both Western states and the Organization of African Unity (OAU) to play a more exacting and proactive role in restoring the economic and political fortunes of the wider continent. There will also be increasing pressure from the same sources to share in peacekeeping/enforcement initiatives, although the precedent set by the botched Lesotho intervention is hardly encouraging. And there is the added difficulty of a Southern African Development Community (SADC) badly divided over the Congo crisis and a solution to it, in the search for which South Africa has wisely decided to invest diplomatic rather than military resources. In these unpropitious circumstances the pace and substance of

[1] *South Africa Year Book* (Pretoria: Government Communication and Information System, 1998), p. 1.
[2] *South African Survey 1997–8* (Johannesburg: South African Institute of Race Relations, 1998), p. 274.

regional integration will be slow and haphazard – a worrying outcome for a government which recognizes the importance of regional associations as a source of protection in a 'new world order' in which the solitary state cannot unilaterally determine its own economic destiny.

Mbeki, however, is likely to emulate his predecessor's active (if at times impetuous) involvement in the formulation and conduct of foreign policy. This is inevitable given his recognition that 'foreign policy begins at home'; and that cutting a figure abroad depends in large part on a sound domestic base, requiring in turn a coherent pattern of external relations in which economic advantage must be given its due weight. This fusion of domestic constraints and external aspirations is one which Mbeki, given his diplomatic skills, knowledge and experience of the world beyond South Africa's borders, is well placed to exploit.

## The future

How different as a whole, therefore, may the Mbeki era prove to be from the Mandela years now ending, particularly in terms of political and economic stability? There will doubtless be some differences on the part of the new government, but perhaps more in style and in operational management than in wholly new directions of policy. Mbeki can scarcely match Mandela's unique prestige and charisma and the problems he inherits may well test him to the limit. Yet he arrives with far more actual experience of governing than Mandela had when he first took over as president. He can be expected to aim at the same type of balancing act when weighing populist demands over such key areas as labour and the economy against the claims of more liberal policies in these fields. At the same time, shifts of emphasis may develop in respect of heightened central control, including some corresponding impatience of opposition, whether nationally or within the ANC alliance. There may be a few surprises, with Mbeki determined to make his own distinctive mark. But the broad approach is likely to remain one of pragmatic if hard-headed government, based upon South Africa's many and varied talents, while seeking gradually to reduce the deep-seated imbalances from South Africa's past.

In short, the 1999 election provides the ANC with a second chance to make good the failures in economic and social performance over the last five years; to strengthen its democratic credentials; to build on the work of the TRC and in the long term 'provide a firmer basis for new national identity within a shared society'. As Mbeki himself emphasizes, 'real reconciliation cannot be achieved without a thorough transformation and democratisation process'. How and with what success he and his government tackle this formidable task will be a central preoccupation for South Africa and its peoples as the country enters the new millennium.

# 2 THE STATE OF THE POLITY

*David Welsh**

## Introduction

The ANC's huge electoral victory in April 1994, when it won 62.7 per cent of the vote, appeared to sceptics to ensure that the South African political system would follow a familiar African sequence: a thumping victory in the founding election, followed by the consolidation of power – and thereafter the steady onset of political sclerosis, as corruption, the abuse of power and economic decline set in.

Many of the ANC's critics maintain that South Africa is destined to follow the trajectories of states like Kenya or Zimbabwe, indeed that there are already portents of the decline of democracy. The critics may be proved right, but this chapter, while not uncritical of the quality of democracy in South Africa nor unmindful of the hazards democracy faces, will suggest less pessimistic possibilities.

The gap between the ANC and the next biggest party, the National Party (NP), which gained 20 per cent of the vote in 1994, is said to be the largest in the democratic world. Added to this is the ANC's victory in seven of the nine provinces and its control of at least two-thirds of the over 800 local authorities. Little is likely to threaten this political hegemony in the 1999 election, in which the only significant issue is whether the ANC will win a two-thirds majority nationally and control of all nine provinces.

The extent to which democracy has been consolidated over the past five years is a moot point. The impeccably liberal-democratic constitution, agreed to in 1996, remains intact. Threats by the Secretary General of the ANC, Kgalema Motlanthe, to limit the independence of the Reserve Bank, the Auditor-General and judiciary should the ANC win a two-thirds majority in 1999 were immediately played down by President Mandela's office, which did, however, acknowledge that the ANC wished to bring greater pressure to bear on those institutions 'so that they transformed in line with government policies'.[1]

* The writer thanks Ken Andrew, Errol Moorcroft, Michael Savage and Virginia van der Vliet for helpful criticism. Factual and ideological errors are the writer's responsibility.
[1] *Business Day* (Johannesburg), 4 May 1998.

**Results of 1994 election**

| Party | % | Seats |
|-------|------|-------|
| ANC   | 62.6 | 252   |
| NP    | 20.4 | 82    |
| IFP   | 10.5 | 43    |
| FF    | 2.2  | 9     |
| DP    | 1.7  | 7     |
| PAC   | 1.2  | 5     |
| ACDP  | 0.5  | 2     |
| Other | 0.9  | 0     |

Total no. of votes cast: 19, 533,498 (86.9 per cent turnout).

Estimated no. of potentially eligible voters in 1999 election: 22.8 million.
SA's population: 41.5 million.

The IEC counted the number of South Africans 18 years and older (as at 28 February 1999), and subtracted from that certain categories of voters who were permitted to vote in 1994: permanent residents (581,000), South African citizens who live overseas permanently (97,000), and South African citizens without bar-coded identity documents (1,358,000). At the time of writing, the status of 150,000 convicted and awaiting-trial prisoners, who were also subtracted, is uncertain. An additional 400,000 17-year-olds who turn 18 before 2 June 1999 were allowed to register, setting the total of eligible voters at 22.8 million. The South African Institute of Race Relations contends that nearly 2 million people have lost their right to vote on 2 June as a result of changes in criteria and documentation requirements.

Some evidence of the extent to which a democratic political culture has put down roots can be gleaned from recent survey data. Polls conducted for the Institute for Democracy in South Africa (IDASA) reveal that while 'steadfast commitment' to democracy is relatively low it has moved in a very encouraging direction in the first few years of South Africa's transition. The 1997 IDASA survey asked respondents: 'If a non-elected government or leader could impose law and order and deliver houses and jobs' how willing they would be 'to give up regular elections and live under such a government'. Only 36 per cent said they would be unwilling, the remainder being 'willing' or 'very willing'.[2] This and other surveys show widespread intolerance of political rivals: over a third of respondents regularly approve of denying basic political rights to 'least-liked' rivals.[3]

Slightly more encouraging findings about the growth of a democratic culture appeared in a Markdata Omnibus survey carried out for the Helen Suzman Foundation

[2] Robert Mattes et al., 'Citizens' Commitment to Democracy', in Wilmot James and Moira Levy (eds), *Pulse: Passages in Democracy-Building – Assessing South Africa's Transition* (Cape Town: IDASA, 1998), pp. 93–4.
[3] Ibid., p. 99.

8

in June 1998. While 49 per cent of respondents thought that the ANC's winning a two-thirds majority would be a good or very good thing (compared with 45 per cent who disagreed), a differently worded question, which included reference to the ANC's ability to change the constitution should it win a two-thirds majority, elicited a different response: no fewer than 60 per cent of respondents, including 53 per cent of African respondents, believed this would be a bad/very bad thing.[4]

The survey data provide a useful context for analysis. Notwithstanding strong anti-democratic undercurrents, the democratic political system, in Przeworski's phrase, has become 'the only game in town'.[5] No significant political force, even putatively secessionist ones such as the rightwing Freedom Front (FF) or a confederalist body such as the Inkatha Freedom Party, seeks to act outside the formal channels of the polity. To this extent stability has been secured, although this by no means precludes politically motivated violence.

Political violence has declined sharply, although it remains at unacceptably high levels. Between September 1984 and December 1997, 23,609 political killings were recorded – an average of nearly 2,000 per annum. For 1996 and 1997, 683 and 470 fatalities occurred, respectively; and a further decline will be recorded for 1998.[6] Most of the violence took place in KwaZulu-Natal. Whether the possible rapprochement between the ANC and the IFP will eliminate the conflict remains doubtful since tensions between the parties remain sharp at the grassroots level and may prove resistant to the urgings of the respective leaderships to cease violence.

## The state of the parties

Given the strength of the ANC and relative weakness of, and divisions among, the opposition parties, the consolidation of the polity as a single-party dominant system is a distinct possibility. The continuing salience of race ensures that the rise of an inter-racial, class-based party that could seriously challenge the ANC is unlikely. Neither the IFP, whose support base is restricted to KwaZulu-Natal, nor the Pan Africanist Congress (PAC) is likely to make significant gains in 1999. Indeed, it is likely that the IFP will lose ground in its stronghold. Despite the legacy of violence between the IFP and the ANC and major policy differences – for instance, concerning the extent of federalism and the status of traditional leaders – it is highly likely that the IFP will remain in government as a (voluntary) coalition partner after the 1999 elections. Speculation suggests that the ANC might offer Mangosuthu Buthelezi, the IFP leader, a deputy presidency.

[4] Helen Suzman Foundation, press release, 27 August 1998.
[5] Adam Przeworski, *Democracy and the Market: Political and Economic Reforms in Eastern Europe and Latin America* (Cambridge: Cambridge University Press, 1991), p. 26.
[6] *South Africa Survey 1997/98* (Johannesburg: South African Institute of Race Relations, 1998), p. 51.

The United Democratic Movement (UDM), which was founded by Bantu Holomisa and Roelf Meyer in 1997, is unlikely to win more than five per cent of the overall vote. Holomisa, a former military ruler of the Transkei 'homeland' and a deputy minister in Mandela's cabinet, was a popular figure among the ANC grassroots until his expulsion in 1996. He may be able to capitalize on popular discontents in the problem-wracked Eastern Cape and in other areas where there are significant numbers of Transkeian migrants.

The New National Party (NNP), led by Marthinus van Schalkwyk, and the Democratic Party, led by Tony Leon, both suffer the burden of being 'historically white' parties which participated in apartheid's political structures. Indeed, the NNP, despite van Schalkwyk's efforts, has been unable to rid itself of the incubus of being the 'apartheid party'. Since much of the political debate harks back to the apartheid past and how that past created the problems with which the ANC is now saddled, it is hard to foresee the NNP's becoming the nucleus of a new opposition party capable of defeating the ANC.

The DP has provided lively opposition in parliament, and Tony Leon has distinguished himself as a fearless critic of government. The DP, however, has been unable to tap significant support in the African, Coloured and Indian electorates. It performed disastrously in the 1994 elections (1.7 per cent of the vote) but, according to survey data, it has significantly improved its position even to the extent of mounting a serious challenge to the NNP's position as the second biggest party.

'Race' trumped all other potential sources of voter preferences in 1994; there is little reason to suppose that matters will be different in 1999. Attempts to downplay the salience of race and to interpret voting behaviour as an expression of 'interests' are unpersuasive: racial divisions reflect the long history of conflict and encapsulate interests, including class interests. The rapid expansion of an African middle class since 1994 is unlikely to change voting patterns. The vast majority of Africans will vote for a 'historically African' party (overwhelmingly the ANC), and conversely, the vast majority of whites will vote for a 'historically white' party (the NNP or the DP). Most Coloured and Indian voters supported the NP in 1994 in what was probably a case of 'better-the-devil-you-know-than-the-devil-you-don't'. They are likely to do the same in 1999.[7]

The comparative study of the politics of divided societies shows that 'winner-takes-all', adversarial politics are fatal to sustaining a credibly democratic political system. In terms of the interim constitution, under which the 1994 elections were contested, provision was made for a Government of National Unity (GNU) representing, proportionately, all parties that won ten per cent or more of the overall vote. The GNU cabinet was to take decisions by consensus.[8]

[7] According to a Markdata poll published in *Rapport*, 29 November 1998.
[8] David Welsh, 'Coalition Government: An Unwilling Marriage?', in Bertus de Villiers (ed.), *State of the Nation 1997/8* (Pretoria: Human Sciences Research Council, 1998).

The institution of the GNU and the (apparently) federal provisions of the interim constitution significantly broke with the 'winner-takes-all' style and eased the transition by lowering the stakes of the founding election. Constitutionally required coalitions, however, have nowhere succeeded, at least as permanent institutions. The GNU, from which the NP withdrew in 1996, was no exception, although the IFP has lasted the full course, with three cabinet portfolios, including Home Affairs which is held by Buthelezi.

The absence of any comparable mechanism in the final constitution and the absence of any significant federal element in the polity suggest that there are few brakes on 'winner-takes-all' politics, except for the electoral system, which is simple proportional representation by list voting.

Aside from the purely institutional features, there is another powerful force at work that militates against a more consensual style of politics: this is the inherent tendency of liberation movements to present themselves as the (sole) voice of 'the people'. In a perceptive article Marina Ottaway compared the ANC with other African liberation movements, and concluded that, like them, the ANC would find it impossible to transform itself into a political party functioning in a competitive multiparty system:

> What characterised liberation movements ... was the stress on unity, the rejection of partisan divisions as destructive of the new nation, and the illusion that an entire country could have a single purpose and accept a single representative to speak as the 'mouthpiece of an oppressed nation'. Political parties operating in a democratic framework, on the other hand, do not pretend to represent a people or a nation, but specific constituencies.[9]

The ANC has declined to describe itself as a party, and insists on retaining its designation as a liberation movement. Yet it would be premature to conclude that the ANC will necessarily follow the common African trajectory and degenerate into an authoritarian system. It has avoided espousing a narrow 'Africanism' in response to white racism, and continues to subscribe to the Freedom Charter's claim that 'South Africa belongs to all who live in it, black and white ...'; but its commitment to non-racialism is qualified by (critics would say 'negated by') an insistence that racial inequalities cannot be addressed other than by continuing attention to race. As Kader Asmal, Minister of Water Affairs and Forestry, put it:

> To pretend to be 'colour blind' is to continue the pattern of inequality, lack of access and exclusion. How can racial wrongs be put right without appropriate emphasis on race?[10]

[9] Marina Ottaway, 'Liberation Movements and Transition to Democracy: the Case of the A.N.C.', *Journal of Modern African Studies*, 29, 1 (1991), p. 66.
[10] Speech in National Assembly, 10 February 1998.

Asmal's rhetorical question explains the explicit use of racial categories (as, for example, in the Employment Equity Act of 1998) that has led critics like the DP to accuse the ANC of 're-racializing' society. Tony Leon has commented that:

> when transformation becomes cloaked by euphemistic clouds of racial quotas and group preference we lose our way and begin following the path of our apartheid past. Apartheid was, in essence, after all, a race-based affirmative-action programme.[11]

Whatever the wisdom of the instruments used, transformation will be the key theme of Thabo Mbeki's presidency. In a series of striking speeches he has stressed the possible explosive consequence of the failure to transform. Only when transformation has been effected will 'true and permanent reconciliation' be possible, and South Africans will cease 'to define ourselves in politics and economics in terms of race, colour and ethnicity'.[12]

Retaining the designation of a liberation movement and defining the principal goal as transformation has facilitated other distinctive features of the ANC's approach to politics. First, liberation movements tend to have a single focus on 'liberation': the ANC, to quote Nelson Mandela's description, is a 'broad church' embracing a wide spread of ideological positions. This has two consequences, one direct and the other indirect.

The 'broad church', by definition, is ideologically diffuse, and it can (apparently) easily accommodate as alliance partners organizations with a very distinctive ideology, such as the South African Communist Party or the Congress of South African Trade Unions. Liberation struggles tolerate internal ideological divisions; governments are far more constrained in their ability to do so. This points to the bind in which the ANC leadership has found itself: it espouses the Growth, Employment and Redistribution programme (GEAR) as fundamental policy – only to have it rejected by its alliance partners (and, no doubt, by a significant number of ANC grassroots activists). This has led to the extraordinary situation in which organized business is more in agreement with the ANC leadership about GEAR than the ANC is with its allies – and this in spite of a pervasive suspicion of (white) business in ANC circles.

The indirect consequence derives from the liberation movement's historic *raison d'être*. In the ANC's case this was opposition to racial discrimination, which gave it cohesiveness. How, though, is cohesiveness to be maintained when that goal has, seemingly, been achieved? Partly by continuing to whip up feelings about the oppressive past, and partly by attacking the white minority for supposedly refusing to support transformation because it endangers their ill-gotten privileges. The pro-

[11] Tony Leon, *Hope and Fear: Reflections of a Democrat* (Johannesburg: Jonathan Ball Publishers, 1998), p. 231.
[12] Thabo Mbeki, *Africa – The Time Has Come: Selected Speeches* (Cape Town: Tafelberg Publishers/ Mafube, 1998), p. 64.

ceedings of the Truth and Reconciliation Commission have been useful in ensuring that the atrocities of the apartheid past have been kept in the public gaze.

That apartheid's legacy has left the new rulers with daunting problems is beyond dispute; that memories of apartheid should still be alive – and painful – is not surprising. The danger is that harking back to the past and invoking apartheid's sins as an all-purpose excuse for policy failure has become a standard reflex for many ANC politicians. Deflecting responsibility for incompetence, unfortunately, is a response that is disempowering.

A second distinctive feature of liberation movement politics exemplified by the ANC is the refusal to respect some of the precepts of constitutional democracy, such as preserving inviolate the line between party and state. Bureaucratic, judicial and parastatal appointments have been routinely given to ANC cadres. There are two mutually reinforcing reasons for this. First, many in the ANC are inclined to scoff at the state/party distinction as a piece of bourgeois delusion (which, in any case, was systematically disregarded under NP rule) that ignores the urgent need for trans-formation, the importance of which far outweighs any concern for constitutional scruples. Secondly, the ANC, understandably, has been apprehensive about a bureaucracy that was dominated by white, Afrikaner males appointed under the old order. It has also questioned the legitimacy of a judiciary in which no more than about 30 judges out of a total of approximately 175 are other than white. While no exact figures have been furnished, perhaps half of the directors-general of national departments are ANC appointees. A similar figure is probably true of other managerial-level appointees in the bureaucracy.

Other highly significant political appointments are the designation of Tito Mboweni, formerly Minister of Labour, as Governor of the Reserve Bank; and the appointment of Bulelani Ngcuka, former chief whip of the ANC in the National Council of Provinces (NCOP), to the newly-created post of national director of public prosecutions. In both cases legitimate fears have been expressed about the independence of these officials from the political executive.

In the circumstances of the transition it was perhaps inevitable that the line between party and state would be blurred. Whether the *de facto* politicization of putatively neutral institutions can be reversed over time or whether they will degenerate into gigantic sources of patronage are worrying issues.


## Governance

Hopes that South Africa would move in a more federal direction have not received much encouragement. In some respects the language of the constitution appeared to suggest federal possibilities, and powers of major importance were assigned to be shared between the national and provincial governments. In practice, however, the experience of the past five years has shown a political system with only federal fig-leaves. The reality is an essentially unitary system with some administrative decentralization. The ANC has never favoured federalism, in which it saw either a backdoor way of giving respectability to reintegrated homelands or the creation of launch-pads for possible secessionist/balkanization attempts. The IFP's mobilization of Zulu ethnicity in KwaZulu-Natal confirmed the ANC's suspicions, and strengthened a conviction that provinces must be kept, politically and financially, on a tight rein.

Further considerations also militated against federalism in the ANC's thinking. Wealthier provinces might use federal arrangements as a shield against ANC-inspired redistributive policies; moreover, the ANC leadership soon became aware that provincial formations inside the ANC engaged in embarrassing public quarrels which the national leadership had to resolve. Some in the ANC may have recognized that a common consequence of federalisation is the concomitant federalization of the parties operating the system. This was a development that the ANC would not tolerate. Liberation movements, virtually by definition, feature strongly centralized leadership, perhaps even 'democratic centralism'.

Strongly centralized control was given further impetus by the acute shortage of ANC leaders with managerial and administrative skills, especially at provincial and local levels.

Neither provincial government nor the National Council of Provinces can be deemed a success after five years of operation. In most, though not all, of the provinces the quality of administration has been poor, if not appalling. Where provinces have been cobbled together out of former homelands – as in Eastern Province, Mpumalanga and Northern Province – problems have been especially acute. Homeland administrations were generally bloated, inefficient and endemically corrupt, but they had to be incorporated holus-bolus into the new administrative set-up because of an agreement reached at the Multiparty Negotiating Process in 1993 that there would be no retrenchment of the civil service for a period of five years, beginning in 1994.

The reason behind this deal was ostensibly a concession by the ANC (a so-called 'sunset' clause) to allay the fears of white civil servants. The ANC believed they constituted an entrenched class of politically powerful conservatives whose non-cooperation could jeopardize the transition. No less true, however, were ANC fears of the political backlash that might be caused by retrenchment among several thousand supernumerary homeland bureaucrats.

The consequence has been the inheritance by the new government of a public service of 1.2 million persons, which is numerically too big for a state of South Africa's size. According to Trevor Manuel, the Minister of Finance, the state could be spending as much as R2 billion per annum on officials whose jobs were superfluous to needs: 'We can't cut housing and education spending just to keep a huge

14

public service employed.'[13] Official policy has been simultaneously to downsize the public service by 300,000 and to ensure that it becomes (racially) representative.

A White Paper issued in April 1998 said the current targets – that 50 per cent of the public service at managerial level must be black, and 30 per cent women – did not represent the ultimate goal – that all groups and levels within the bureaucracy should be racially representative of society as a whole.[14]

By the end of 1998, these targets had almost been reached, according to the Department of Public Service and Administration. By the beginning of that year only 19.24 per cent of all public service officials were white, a drop of 8.32 per cent per annum since 1994 when the figure was 44 per cent. Over 56 per cent of directors-general and their deputies and 41 per cent of other management posts came from 'previously disadvantaged communities'.[15]

Since public servants could not suffer retrenchment, the government had recourse to other means of expediting the departure of whites, notably by offering generous severance packages and not filling vacancies. By early 1998, 48,000 individual packages had been granted, half to whites.[16] To some extent, however, the scheme backfired since many of those taking packages were more experienced and competent officials whom the public service could not afford to lose.[17] In general, morale among white public servants has declined, and few young whites now con-template a career in the public service since affirmative action is widely considered to impose a ceiling on their chances of promotion.

Similar changes have taken place in the South African National Defence Force (SANDF). Only one per cent of officers in the apartheid Defence Force were black; by 1998, according to Ronnie Kasrils, the Deputy Minister of Defence, the figure had risen to 29 per cent. Some 30,000 members of the liberation movements' guerrilla forces have been integrated into the SANDF, which is currently headed by a former Umkhonto we Sizwe soldier, General Siphiwe Nyanda.[18]

## Corruption

Serious questions arise in relation to the efficiency of the public service and the extent of corruption. With disarming candour, President Nelson Mandela informed the NCOP in August 1998 that government today was being run by:

[13] *Cape Argus* (Cape Town), 7–8 February 1998.
[14] *Business Day*, 28 April 1998.
[15] *Die Burger* (Cape Town), 1 December 1998.
[16] *South Africa Survey* 1997/8, p. 484.
[17] Department of Public Service and Administration, *The Provincial Review Report* (Cape Town, 1997), p. 37.
[18] *The Sowetan* (Johannesburg), 31 August 1998.

men and women who have been taken literally from the bush and without previous training, and they have been asked to run the government of such a highly developed country as South Africa. Our white compatriots have had the advantage, which has been denied to us, of going to school and university, getting training, and acquiring knowledge, skills and expertise.[19]

The President's point may be well taken, but it does not dispose of the problem that good governance is impossible without a reasonably efficient bureaucracy. It is in the provinces, which employ 60 per cent of public servants, that the problems of poor administrative capacity are most acute. The Provincial Review Report, published by the Department of Public Service and Administration in 1997, is a litany of malpractice, lack of skills and poor cooperation between national and provincial departments.

The report is too lengthy and too detailed to summarize adequately. Given the growing seriousness of corruption, it is, however, worthwhile to quote its finding on financial management:

> There is a tendency, in many provinces, to delegate responsibility for financial administration and control as far as possible ... decentralisation not adequately supported by the provision of competent staff, spells disaster. There is a serious shortage of well qualified and trained financial management staff in most of the provinces. Staff in departmental Finance components are of a low rank. At the same time, senior managers in departments do not appear to have the knowledge or appreciation for good financial management and efficient administration. .... In major spending departments such as Education and Health unqualified finance personnel are administering budgets of billions.[20]

Similar comments about the quality of financial controls in national departments have regularly been voiced by the Auditor-General, sometimes to the discomfiture and anger of the responsible ministers.

It is impossible to quantify the amounts appropriated by corruption in the public and private sectors. South Africa is a country with a very poor tax morality and, combined with the large-scale evasion of customs duties, probably at least R30 billion escapes the state's revenue net annually.

It is not a rewarding exercise to compare levels of corruption in the 'old' South Africa and the 'new'. Apartheid itself was a gigantic form of racial nepotism and therefore qualifies as inherently corrupt. Arms embargoes, oil and other sanctions were also conducive to heightened corruption since devious ways of circumventing them were necessary. A lack of transparency and accountability, as well as a severely

[19] Speech in National Council of Provinces, 7 August 1998.
[20] *Provincial Review Report*, p. 40.

controlled press, ensured that little light was shed on the dark places in which corruption flourished.

Corruption remains a serious problem and a threat to democracy. It is to the credit of the ANC's leadership that it is aware of this and does not hesitate to lash out against those, including ANC members, who engage in corrupt behaviour. Thabo Mbeki, in particular, is likely to make an attack on corruption one of the key elements of his presidency. Having been in exile elsewhere in Africa for many years he saw at first hand exactly how corrosive of effective governance corruption is. At an Anti-Corruption Summit Conference in Cape Town in November 1998 Mbeki used unprecedentedly strong language:

> The culture of entitlement, so prevalent in our community, has contributed to the 'name it, claim it' syndrome where individuals seek an elusive moral justification for engaging in criminal activity. The crisis in public values is visible in the lack of professional conduct from so many wearing the badge of public honour in the civil service. … The illusion of the sumptuous life made possible by profits from illicit practices has taken its toll on the very proponents of the new order, one that was meant to be built on the ruins of apartheid.[21]

However seriously intended, strictures are not enough to curb evils. Critics of the ANC have commonly maintained that the ANC excels at framing plans or programmes – but falls down in implementing them. Its ability to clamp down on corruption remains in doubt.

*Effectiveness*

This possibility introduces another dimension of governance that is critical to the future: does South Africa have an *effective* state, or are symptoms of the *soft* state emerging? Apart from such weaknesses as inefficient tax and customs duties collection, a number of other disquieting indicators exist. The most serious of these is the apparent inability of the state to control crime or bring criminals to book. According to data released by the police, only one in every seven murders reported ends in a conviction; and only one in 50 car hijackings results in a conviction. Comparably dismal figures exist for other (common) crimes such as armed robbery and car theft.[22] Crime rates are exacerbated by easy access to illegal guns, of which between three and four million are estimated to be in circulation.

Another telling example relates to traffic: even the most casual observer of South African driving habits quickly appreciates the extent of lawlessness on the roads:

[21] *Cape Argus*, 11 November 1998.
[22] *Business Day*, 14 January 1999.

17

nearly 10,000 people die annually in crashes (many more than the number of victims of political violence); perhaps as many as 10 per cent of all drivers either do not have or have fraudulently acquired driving licences; and, according to the Minister of Transport, nearly 60 per cent of all traffic fines are never paid.[23]

A prospective example of state incapacity is likely to be the implementation of the Employment Equity Act, which prescribes affirmative action targets for all firms that meet certain criteria of size and turnover. At least 10,000 firms will be liable to the legislation. Only the most sanguine of observers would believe that the legislation is capable of enforcement, while the suspicious-minded fear that it may be selectively enforced against firms that the state, for whatever reason, decides to target.

No discussion of South Africa's prospects should omit reference to the AIDS epidemic. Here, too, the state has failed to promote safer sex campaigns effectively. More than 1,500 South Africans a day are infected with HIV, and an estimated three million have already been infected. Mary Crewe comments on a recent government initiative:

> The government gave no vision, no inspiration, no plans and no leadership. Nothing beyond vague generalities that have been placed on the agenda for over a decade.[24]

There are indications that Thabo Mbeki, who will assume the presidency after the election, is determined to confront the problem of the ineffective state, including, as was shown, corruption. Mbeki is more of a manager than Mandela ever was. In the two years or so in which Mbeki has assumed *de facto* control of government he has taken a firmer grip of the state's machinery, as well as centralizing control of the ANC. More strongly centralized control, however, may alienate those elements of the ANC, notably COSATU and the internal mass opposition of the 1980s, who demand exhaustive consultation before any policy initiative.

The dangers of the single-party dominant system are real, but it must be remembered that, as yet, South Africa has neither deeply-rooted democratic institutions nor a resilient political culture that could cope with the (hypothetical) alternation of governments via the ballot box. A powerful case can be made for the view that stability is best maintained by a secure government that is neither tempted into rash populist measures nor paralysed by the possibility of losing power, but is confident enough to implement necessary, but painful, economic reforms.

'Secure' government, however, by no means assures good government. Too much 'security' encourages precisely those debilitating characteristics mentioned at the beginning of this chapter. If single-party dominance is inevitable in the medium term (10 to 15 years), it will hopefully be tempered and restrained by constitutional

[23] *Die Burger*, 20 November 1998.
[24] Mary Crewe, 'Reflections on the Partnership Against AIDS', *AIDS Bulletin*, 17, 3, December 1998, p. 5.

checks and balances, a lively opposition, even if small, a free press and a vigorous civil society. South Africa scores reasonably well on each of these indicators.

The ANC has been accused of imposing a 'creeping hegemony' – and there are disquieting signs of a tendency to 'interference by government in every sphere of life' (to quote Steve Tshwete, the Minister of Sport and Recreation). The press remains free, even though some of the mainstream English-language newspapers are poor in quality and are inclined to be toadying in their attitude to government. The (overwhelmingly white) private sector, while opposed to recent labour legislation, has been muted in its criticism. Business is aware of lingering suspicions of its bona fides in ANC ranks, and, accordingly, avoids public confrontation as far as possible.

## Conclusion

Over the past five years a frequent lament of the ANC has been that 'we are in office but not in power'. The lament appears to refer to the relatively weak economic power of Africans, and the conversely formidable power of the predominantly white private sector, along with remaining white influence in the bureaucracy, the judiciary, the media, the universities and other formations of civil society.

Little can be done about these asymmetries of power in the short run without crude social engineering that would likely cripple the country. South Africa's stability rests upon a tacit trade-off between the political power of the majority as represented by the ANC, and the economic and social power of the minority. Heribert Adam and his co-authors observe that South Africa is 'a pragmatically united rather than a deeply divided society.'[25] It is surely both.

[25] Heribert Adam, F. van Zyl Slabbert and Kogila Moodley, *Comrades in Business: Post-Liberation Politics in South Africa* (Cape Town: Tafelberg Publishers, 1997), p. 158.

# 3 THE ANC AND BLACK POLITICS: THE BUCK STOPS WITH MBEKI

*Stanley Uys*

While President Nelson Mandela has concerned himself with ceremonial matters, and winning foreign friends and influencing people, Deputy President Thabo Mbeki has been running South Africa: chairing the cabinet, managing day-to-day affairs, shaping short- and long-term policies, and moving on to the wider African stage as a visionary-extraordinary. Yet the question is still asked: what will happen when Mandela goes?

Professor Heribert Adam, a seasoned observer, thinks the question is silly, because it personalizes and attributes the country's 'miracle' transition to Mandela's 'reconciling magic'. He remarks: 'While Mandela's exemplary role in marketing the historic compromise must be fully credited, it reveals the political illiteracy of trembling investors who think that the "miracle" could or would be undone after the source of divine inspiration has disappeared.'[1]

Another way of looking at the political changeover is to ask whether Mbeki can hold the black centre together without Mandela's assistance (assuming Mandela feels disposed to assist him). This is a critical juncture for Mbeki. National elections, Mandela's departure, and the metamorphosis of the African National Congress from a broad liberation movement to a narrower political party, under a commitment to deliver impossible election promises, have combined to create a natural moment for ANC followers to quit the fold, if they so wish.

The question then is not whether an unknown Mbeki will emerge when Mandela goes, but whether the ANC will become less authoritative as an instrument of governance. Mandela has been not only a reconciler, but also, within the ANC, a disciplinarian. As a continuing ex-officio member of the ANC's National Executive Committee, and a party grandee, he may still be able to support Mbeki after the elections; but already, as he steps down from Camelot into the muddy waters of internal ANC politics, the famous 'Madiba' authority is waning. So Mbeki is on his own.

The question is: how will Mbeki structure his presidency for the daunting task ahead? Already, there are clear indicators that, unlike the more laid-back Mandela

[1] *Indicator South Africa*, University of Natal, autumn 1997.

presidency, it will be a more centralized, decisive, even authoritarian, presidency. Not only enemies, but ordinary political opponents, will be given short shrift, as Mbeki tailors his presidency to control an unschooled black constituency.

## Reconciliation on the back burner

ANC priorities have changed since 1994. Reconciliation between blacks and whites is just not a current preoccupation. Reconciliation steered the country around a possible Afrikaner revolt, saw the ANC safely through the transition, and conferred on Mandela and ex-President F. W. de Klerk the Nobel Peace prizes they richly deserved. Now blacks will surge towards what they regard as their due rewards, edging whites, coloureds and Indians (even within the ANC) to the sidelines.

Much of the reconciliation achieved in 1994 has been overtaken by indifference among blacks and alienation among whites. The Truth and Reconciliation Commission was of momentous historical importance in revealing much of the truth, but as an exercise in reconciliation it was a non-starter. As Mbeki himself said, as recently as November 1998, South Africa remains 'a deeply divided nation'.

When the 1994 elections were held, racial animosities were not an active factor. Whites mistakenly thought reconciliation represented the full extent of transition, while the patience and goodwill shown by black voters were the patience and good-will of victors-designate. In 1994, black expectations were in waiting mode, but since securing political control blacks are turning their expectations towards economic 'transformation', whatever this might turn out to be. The buck stops with Mbeki.

The low level of black triumphalism in the 1994 elections was deceptive. Whites, beguiled by the offer of a government of national unity, kept a low profile, and blacks, with the self-confidence of numbers, could afford to be relaxed about the voting outcome. They would not merely win power through the ANC – there was no runner-up.

In a population of just under 41 million, blacks count for about 31 million or 76.7 per cent (whites are 11 per cent, Coloureds 9 per cent and Indians/Asians 3 per cent); in the 1994 elections they polled 73 per cent of the total vote and 94 per cent of the ANC vote, which in itself was 62.65 per cent of the total vote; and at the ANC's key national conference on 16 December 1997, 96 per cent of the 3,000-plus delegates were blacks.

## The rot of 'careerism'

This chapter will explore just how much reliance the ANC leadership can place on post-election black support. While the ANC's re-election to office is assured, mainly through the magic of its name (its majority may even be greater), after the elections the momentum of 'liberation' will steadily exhaust itself.

At the ANC's 1997 conference, Mandela identified 'careerism' – a catch-all word – as a central weakness. Since 1994, it had 'created such problems as division within the movement, conflicts based on differences among individuals, the encouragement of rank indiscipline leading to the undermining of our organizational integrity, conflict within communities and the demoralization of some of the best cadres'.[2] Surveying the numerous black organizations seeking part of post-liberation action – youth, students, non-governmental organisations (NGOs), community-based organizations (CBOs), sport, culture, religion, tribal – Mandela added:

> Many of these organizations ... have degenerated into nothing more than special interest groups, whose task is to access the limited pool of public resources to advance their own interests. ... Many have taken pride in assuming positions of militant opposition to the very government they put in power, solely for the purpose of advancing their own self-interests, completely detached from the overall and global objectives which the progressive movement as a whole must seek to achieve.

Mbeki sent out the same signal in the ANC's traditional 8 January birthday message when he vowed to kick corrupt 'careerists' out of the ANC and out of government. They were in government, he said, because they wanted money, not to serve the nation. 'We find these enemies of the people throughout the structures of government, from the local to the national level.'

The post-election challenge to the Mbeki presidency then will be to retain black political support while economic solutions (hopefully) unfold, and vice versa. The ANC leadership's concern over the free-for-all within party ranks may appear exaggerated to the outsider, but opinion polls point repeatedly to a growing drift away from the black centre. Also, a number of internal party problems seem to be causing deep anxiety. The hypersensitivity shown sometimes by ANC leaders to criticism may be more a product of these difficulties than an incipient 'authoritarianism'.

Mandela offered one explanation for his apprehensions: 'Because we have just begun, the process of fundamental social transformation has not yet impacted seriously on the apartheid paradigm, which affects all aspects of our lives. This process therefore has not yet tested the strength of the counter-offensive which would seek to maintain privileges of the white minority.' This seems implausible. While the white, Coloured and Indian minorities probably could restrain the government's free hand, a 'counter-offensive' is just not within their reach. Whites who can afford to quit the country would do so, rather than fight.

[2] ANC document, 16 December 1997.

A more credible explanation of Mandela's and Mbeki's unease is Mandela's concern that, without 'transformation', there could be a 'political explosion' among blacks, and Mbeki's warning that 'The combination of abject poverty at one end and a comfortable affluence at the other end, compounded by the fact that this describes a black-white divide … constitutes an explosive mixture'.[3] Mbeki speaks even of 'mounting rage' and 'race riots'. This shows the government's real fear, which is not over what whites might do, but over what blacks might do.

## The 'broad church' breaks up

The seeds of the ANC's internal conflicts lie in its 87-year history as a 'broad church', encompassing a range of black opinion, from radical leftists to conservative Christians. ANC leaders would like to maintain this wide catchment, but the 'broad church' is starting to break up.

The ANC's fundamental weakness is lack of organizational cohesion. Banned from 1960 to 1990, it was unable to create a conventional party structure with the usual branches, lines of command, acknowledged hierarchy, disciplinary framework and checks and balances – the pecking order without which no party can be stable. It is unlikely that Mbeki wants a vibrant grassroots organization able to challenge party headquarters at every turn, but he must surely want something more solid and predictable in its processes than the present scramble.

In Mandela's words, ANC men and women were 'taken literally from the bush'. They had no experience of high government or parliamentary office. Their entry into power in 1994 was 'unplanned and disorganized'. The party 'behaved in a manner that could have endangered the revolution'.

A strong concept of leadership is missing among ANC followers. Most of the party's leaders were in prison or exile during the three decades of illegality (1960–90), and their surrogates in the 1980s, including the United Democratic Front (UDF) and Mass Democratic Movement (MDM), kept their leaderships mobile to stay ahead of the security police, with the result that the idea of leadership receded to the point of being tenuous.

Since its unbanning, the ANC – generally seen to be dominated by former exiles and Robben Island prisoners – has had difficulty maintaining, or recasting to its satisfaction, relations with former allies and tributaries. This includes particularly the UDF/MDM which, under ANC pressure, resentfully closed shop in the early 1990s.

Other indicators of internal ANC problems are: the decline of opposition to apartheid as a source of cohesion; the way in which the ANC's admirable principles of non-racialism have weakened black nationalism, creating a vacuum for rivals – a

[3] WOZA (www.woza.co.za) on-line news service, Cape Town, 11 November 1998.

debility Mbeki's Africanism may well be devised to address; and a backlash against an emergent 'liberation aristocracy', seen to benefit unduly from patronage.

As for tribalism, South Africa's new constitution recognizes 'the institution, status and role of traditional leadership', but post-1994 modernized local government structures encroach on tribal powers, and impatient young blacks push for chiefs and headmen to be scrapped. In retaliation, for example in areas such as the Eastern Cape province, chiefs may influence their followers to vote against the ANC.

## NGOs and the youth

ANC relationships with non-governmental organizations, thousands of which were active in the anti-apartheid struggle, generally have deteriorated. Many foreign donations have been diverted to the central government, but also political divisions have arisen with NGOs. The South African National Civic Organization (SANCO), for example, once a natural support base of the ANC, is fractured into different camps. Some NGOs have aspirations, collectively, to become South Africa's 'fourth pillar', alongside government, business and labour. This is the last thing the ANC leadership wants to hear.

Simultaneously, the ANC is reaping the harvest of its 1980s exhortation to the black youth to make South Africa ungovernable. As Simon Schama noted in *Citizens: A Chronicle of the French Revolution*: 'The dilemma for successive generations of those politicians who graduated from oratory to administration was that they owed their own power to precisely the kind of rhetoric that made their subsequent governance impossible.' The ANC's dilemma is not as acute as this, but Mandela and Mbeki regularly have to remind the youth now that their futures lie in post-1994 'transformation', not in persisting with the pre-1994 'struggle'.

In some universities, when demands have been refused, rogue students have gone on the rampage. In August last year, Mbeki lost patience:

> Universities are not a site of struggle, but a site of learning. ... We must get ... out of our minds that there are inexhaustible funds of public finances immediately to redress the gross imbalances we inherited from the apartheid years. When I have asked the question of some of the student organizations that attach to themselves the label 'progressive' what they are doing to contribute to the reconstruction and development of our country, the response has been a deafening silence, broken only by the sound of the toyi-toyi and the sickening chant – give me this! give me that! give me the other!

Some students, said Mbeki, 'entertain the false notion that the democratic order provides an opportunity for licentious conduct and a collapse of social and individual discipline.'[4]

[4] ANC News Briefs, 31 August 1998.

The nine provincial governments are a source of perennial concern to ANC headquarters, where they are seen as another centrifugal force. Although South Africa is a unitary state, there is a constant tug-of-war as the provinces seek more devolved powers – to further not only federal ideas, but factionalism and personal power bases. The National Council of Provinces (the second parliamentary chamber) is a half-baked idea, and an expensive one, not designed to benefit the central party.

## Whither the tripartite alliance?

Most of these weakening relationships eventually will find their own level, but the ominous cloud on the ANC's horizon is its Tripartite Alliance with the South African Communist Party/Congress of South African Trade Unions. The conflict here centres on GEAR, the ANC's IMF-friendly, 1996 macro-economic policy document, which as the 'socialist' SACP/COSATU see it holds South Africa in thrall to capitalism's 'global economics'.

At the annual conferences of these two partners last year, Mandela and Mbeki spelt out the ground rules: toe the ANC line – or quit. All three partners are campaigning now for an ANC victory, but after the elections tensions can be expected to return, particularly if, as Mbeki has hinted, the government moves to deregulate a rigid labour market to promote job creation.

COSATU, the country's biggest trade union federation (1.8 million affiliated members), would be the greater loss to the ANC, because it can mobilize votes. Yet, however much the ANC would miss COSATU's input, it will not allow (in Mandela's words) some members to assert a leadership role 'separate and apart from and in some instances in contradiction with the rest of the political leadership of our own broad democratic movement'.

The SACP has less to offer, except through its strong COSATU links. It claims a membership of 80,000, up to 80 of the 252 ANC MPs, five cabinet ministers and key office-holders in black unions. Over the decades, the SACP has made an indispensable contribution to the ANC, but its strength derives now from 'entryism', or infiltration into strategic positions, and the more the ANC reserves these positions now for its own loyalists, the more the SACP will find itself knocking at a closed door.

The fault line in the alliance is obvious: how can two of the three partners reject the linchpin of ANC policy, GEAR? And how do voters know which candidates stand for what on parliamentary and provincial lists that do not indicate other affiliations?

## Sifting the candidates

The ANC's choice of national and provincial election candidates is based on the party list system introduced in 1994, giving the leadership considerable control over nominations. Further, a party 'deployment committee' recommends where cadres should be placed, voluntarily or involuntarily, so that they are most useful, or least troublesome, whether in parliament, provincial legislatures, parastatals or elsewhere.

The nomination lists published in February were masterly in the way they balanced allegiances within the alliance, but they left the thought that if anything happened to the person at the apex (Mbeki), the carefully balanced structure could become unstable.

Another all-important disciplinary instrument, written into the country's constitution, is that, if public representatives lose their party membership (for example through defection), they can be expelled from parliament. Last year, referring to 'traitors, puppets and criminals' in the ANC's midst, Mbeki served notice on dissidents: 'We will be better off if they resigned and joined other organizations where they can pursue their objectives in the midst of kindred spirits.'[5] Mrs Winnie Madikizela-Mandela apparently is not included in this category. Although the ANC's election code stipulates that candidates must have 'no criminal record or a non-political nature', and 'no history of ill-discipline or corruption', she ranked very high (tenth) on the ANC candidates' long list for the June elections.

The election truce agreed in 1998 between the three partners restricted any purge of troublemakers the ANC might have had in mind. Some senior SACP members, who were feeling a chill wind on their backs, have made their peace and will return to parliament as ANC MPs. If they bring forward an internal challenge again, the ANC can take away their parliamentary seats.

If the tripartite alliance splits, the obvious consequence would be the formation of a (black) 'socialist' or workers' party, with COSATU as its core and the SACP making an organizational and ideological input. An SACP theoretician suggests the party should base itself on a populist model, but populism, to the limited extent that it has surfaced in South Africa, takes a wary view of unionized blacks as an elite whose interests do not always correspond with those of the unemployed, rural poor, landless squatters etc.

Forecasting the potential of a 'socialist' movement is guesswork. Its future would depend on the ANC's capacity to meet expectations, and that capacity has still to be tested. Such a movement, too, would be almost wholly uniracial – not a facilitator for the 'new South Africa'.

[5] *Cape Argus,* 12 September 1998.

## Strains within SACP/COSATU

Tensions are evident not only in the ANC/SACP/COSATU alliance, but also within the SACP/COSATU. The prospect of the political wilderness is not an attractive one, so a break with the ANC would be protracted, with the SACP/COSATU in the role of hostages to Mbeki, until the parting of the ways can no longer be delayed.

At the SACP/COSATU conferences in 1998, observers caught a whiff of the way the wind was blowing, with the election of hardliners such as Blade Nzimande, who became SACP general secretary. Significantly, Nzimande is leaving parliament at the elections to give his full energies to making the SACP organizationally powerful enough to survive a future without the ANC. Mbhazima (Sam) Shilowa, COSATU's general secretary and a close associate of Mbeki's, lost his seat on the SACP Politburo, and will now become an ANC MP (or cabinet minister?), leaving the way clear for his deputy, the more militant Zwelinzima Vavi (elected to the SACP Politburo), to replace him.

## Eclipse of the white liberals

Relations between the ANC and white liberals theoretically should be better than with most non-ANC groupings, because they are supposed to share the same values. Yet animosities are fiercer than with anyone else.

The ANC bridles particularly at criticism by what it sees as the white liberal establishment – the South African Institute of Race Relations (SAIRR) and the Helen Suzman Foundation – which charge the ANC with pursuing a single truth, dismissing the idea of a loyal opposition, collapsing party, government and state into one, being over-interventionist, and prone to over-centralization, autocratic rule and intolerance of opposition.

John Kane-Berman, SAIRR executive director, predicts that civil rights will be whittled away in South Africa now, one by one, by democratic process, and in the name of 'transformation'. R.W. Johnson, director of the Helen Suzman Foundation, takes much the same view.

Two ANC discussion papers on 'transformation (one in 1996, the other an update in 1998) have fuelled this conflict with their insistence on ANC control of all the 'levers of power'.

A widely-held opinion in the liberal 'establishment' is that while South Africa has a democratic constitution and elections, the ANC lacks both a democratic mind-set and a genuine commitment to 'constitutional liberalism'. Kane-Berman believes that 'As a society we are in danger of becoming far more stultified intellectually than we were under National Party rule.' He commits the SAIRR to an 'intellectual revolution' against ANC-imposed 'political correctness'.[6]

[6] SAIRR, *Frontiers of Freedom*, first quarter 1999.

The ANC is careful to concede that not all white liberals are hostile, but it accuses many of them of clinging to untenable privileges, being insufferably patronizing, acknowledging ANC achievements only grudgingly, and showing little sympathy for the frustration blacks feel over economic policy.

Although the ANC leadership is no longer 'socialist'-orientated, it seethes when SACP/COSATU activists accuse it of impotence in the face of market economics. Recently relationships have improved with key business organizations, but the ANC feels it is still not persuading enough businesses that they swim or sink with an ANC government.

## The right to oppose

At the ANC's December 1997 conference, Mandela challenged the right of white opposition parties to oppose his government in the style that would be common-place in democracies. These parties, he said,

> have chosen to propagate a reactionary, dangerous and opportunist position which argues that: a normal and stable democracy has been achieved; the apartheid system is a thing of the past; their legitimate responsibility is to oppose us as the majority party, thus to present themselves as elements of a shadow government which has no responsibility both for our past and our present; and consequently that they have a democratic obligation merely to discredit the ruling party so that they may gain power after the next elections ... the issue of how to address commonly defined national objectives in a united manner, while protecting the identities and common appeal of the separate political parties and formations, remains a matter which only the future will be able to resolve. We have failed to achieve this result during the last three years.

This startling proposition – that South Africa is not a stable democracy yet, and therefore not entitled to the luxury of democratic processes, is ominous for the parliamentary opposition, the media, NGOs and others. It is a clear warning that if criticism passes a certain point, it becomes high crimes and misdemeanours. Mandela questioned directly the right of the Democratic Party 'to position itself as an implacable enemy of the ANC', saying the ANC 'must have a two-thirds majority [in the post-election parliament] to ensure that we are not interfered with by [white] Mickey-mouse parties'.[7]

Whether the ANC in fact would significantly alter the constitution is still to be seen, but the symbolism of just achieving such a majority would have a depressant

[7] Reuters, Foreign Correspondents' Association, Cape Town, 11 November 1998.

effect on the opposition, on parliamentary democracy and even on some foreign governments and investors.

Even the small Pan Africanist Congress (PAC) and the Azanian People's Organization (AZAPO) were advised by Mandela to 'abandon the illusion that they are significant factors in the continuing struggle for the genuine liberation of the people'. As for the mass media, its sin is one of 'setting itself up as a force opposed to the ANC'.

Perhaps the frankest statement on the future of the white opposition comes from William Makgoba, professor of immunology at Witwatersrand University and a free-wheeling political pundit, who does not necessarily speak for the ANC:

No matter how one looks at the issues, one comes to the sobering conclusion that unless the African is placed at the centre of the transformation and national agenda, our country will not be stable, productive or competitive. ... The truth and reality in South Africa today and into the future is no longer European or white, but African and more often black. The sooner the opposition parties get this message, the better. The days of white politics, white privilege, white constituency and white truth are over and will never return.

## The new 'Africanism'

The ANC's deference to Chief Mangosuthu Buthelezi, leader of the Inkatha Freedom Party in KwaZulu-Natal (KZN), as the only significant non-ANC participant in this year's elections, is a remarkable turnaround. At the time of writing, the two parties are negotiating an electoral understanding. For 15 years they slaughtered each other on KZN's killing fields. Now Inkatha will continue to serve in the Government of National Unity and Buthelezi may become South Africa's second deputy president.

The immediate effect of an ANC-IFP election pact could well be to reduce ANC-IFP violence in KZN. However, there are two other dimensions. First, there would be symbolical unification of the Nguni-speaking people – Zulus who account for 22 per cent of South Africa's total population and Xhosas for just over 18 per cent. This could provoke a tribal response among non-Nguni groups. Already, the Venda and Shangaan (for different reasons) are restive. If this is Mbeki's new Africanist philosophy in action, it may well provide the ANC not only with the two-thirds majority it wants in parliament, but with the image of a monolith.

The second, important dimension is that with Buthelezi's support Mbeki will find it easier to cut adrift from the SACP/COSATU if they go down the 'socialist' road. Buthelezi makes no secret of his intense dislike of the SACP/COSATU. His aides urge the ANC privately to 'cut off this cancerous limb'.

No crystal ball is needed to see that the 1999 elections will repeat the racial voting pattern of five years ago: the New National Party (NNP) and the Democratic Party (DP) will poll few black votes, and the ANC will poll even fewer white votes; and the more minority groups are marginalized by black numbers, the more the electoral field will become a black monopoly. The ANC would then risk painting itself into a uniracial corner.

## United opposition front?

If politics in South Africa follow this pattern, and minority groups are shut out of mainstream black politics, the devil will find work for idle hands. The smaller parties will have little to do except intensify criticism of the very issues on which the ANC is hypersensitive: 'anti-democratic' trends, intolerance, corruption, nepotism, non-accountability, a lust for power – just when everyone's shoulder should be to the nation-building wheel.

Before long, groupings outside the ANC-Inkatha laager would start to engage one another in talks on a 'united front'. Many such talks have taken place over the past two years, all leading nowhere, because it was necessary first for each party, however small, to test the waters independently.

After the elections, the scene could change. In every country, 'united fronts' are the most elusive of political holy grails. Confronted, however, by an impenetrable government ethnic bloc, opposition groups would either thrash around helplessly on the periphery, or seriously reassess the obstacles to unity. An opposition realignment would require the presence of at least one predominantly black grouping in a leadership role. The PAC and UDM are obvious, if lightweight, candidates, but so would be an emergent black business-professional-intellectual elite, not unduly beholden to ANC patronage.

Such a movement would need to demarcate its difference from the ANC by being overtly non-racial. This means all players would have to discard their loads of political baggage.

## Playing the Africanist card?

If Mbeki is perceived as an Africanist, and this is to be the theme of his presidency, it is because he invited the label with his famous 1996 speech which began 'I am an African ...', and with his premature vision of an 'African Renaissance' (cynics ask 'When was the Naissance?').

Analyst Vincent Maphai insists that Mbeki is not an Africanist 'in an ethnic or racialist sense'. This is a reasoned point. As Professor Robert Schrire (University of Cape Town) notes: 'Whereas most political leaders come to be identified with a

30

faction or ideology, Mbeki's allies range from liberals to Africanists, and from active Marxists to anti-communist members of the newly affluent black elite. He is almost impossible to categorize either politically or ideologically.' Since Mbeki draws on whatever tradition suits him, it is plausible he is playing the Africanist card as a counter to the impatient 'socialism' of the SACP/COSATU.

Mbeki's critics present him as a consummate manipulator, with hidden agendas, cabals, enforcers and hit lists, and brittleness in the face of criticism: an insecure man who pursues power obsessively, yet never succeeds in wholly reassuring himself.

According to Schrire, Mbeki 'views politics as a struggle between enemies rather than a competition between opponents. Policy failures are attributed to conspiracies and hidden dark forces'. Dr Howard Barrell, formerly an ANC member, now a political journalist, says that people 'have, in whispers, raised concerns about the personality Mbeki brings to his high office ... Nobody doubts Mbeki's intellectual equipment ... It is his extraordinary sensitivity ... that is at issue.'

In the view of Douglas Gibson, deputy leader of the Democratic Party, 'Thabo Mbeki seems increasingly to be a peddler of ominous threats and utopian visions ... this is precisely the same ideological cul-de-sac that has taken the rest of Africa down the road of corrupt one-party rule ... there is going to be far too much concentration of power in ANC hands over the next five years. And that power is going to be corrupt and be abused.'

## Realities of power

A number of the institutions and political traditions through which Mbeki must exercise leadership are weak. As a result, just as Mandela personalized ANC politics after 1994, so Mbeki looks like doing the same after 1999. It is important then to understand the man, considered such an 'enigma' by his peers. Is Mbeki an autocrat-in-waiting, or are his 'autocratic' tendencies political – that is, motivated to ensure that the black centre holds – rather than personal in their origins?

The point is: to what purpose is Mbeki centralizing power? Whatever his individual psychological proclivities might be, whatever his high-minded intentions, whatever the provisions of the constitution and the Bill of Rights, the exigencies of 'transformation' (including combating crime) are likely to make South Africa less, not more, democratic (in the civil rights sense) in coming years. As an aide in his office remarked recently: 'Right now, democracy looks like permissiveness, anarchy and lawlessness. People are lazing about, civil servants don't work, everyone expects something for nothing. We are going to enforce discipline. Things are going to change. We mean business.'[8]

[8] WOZA (www.woza.co.za), Cape Town, 5 February 1999.

Debating Mbeki's personality is one of South Africa's popular pastimes. Surprisingly, although his office has been vastly expanded, his media relations remain very weak, and this hampers a proper appraisal of him. Mbeki has more than his fair share of enemies, but recurrent criticism needs to be balanced by undoubted credits: a genuine passion to see an African rebirth, unwavering commitment to GEAR, a determined attempt to reshape the ANC as an effective instrument of governance, personal incorruptibility, acute political instincts, and – more recently – moving towards a more coherent foreign policy.

Accepting for the moment that Mbeki is creating a one-party-dominant state: is that dominance to be permanent, or is it a first step towards opening the power base to the rest of the country? In whom should South Africans place their trust: Mbeki the autocrat, for whom black power is an end in itself, or Mbeki the democrat, for whom black power is the route to the 'rainbow nation'? The jury is still out.

The imperative of Africanization (in South Africa, the immediate cutting edge of Africanism) cannot be questioned. The point is how it will be implemented: will it enhance or diminish Mbeki's capacity to deliver 'transformation'?

The probability is that, if transformation fails, the ANC would further castigate whites, which would discourage business expansion and thereby job creation (since whites are still commercially dominant), and this in turn would encourage the already serious drift towards emigration, creating a downward spiral, with the country shedding indispensable managerial and other skills. The notion that transformation can be achieved just by voting money has been shown to be an illusion – expenditure becomes a bottomless pit. Are Africanism and nation-building then mutually exclusive, or can Mbeki harness them in a team?

Whatever conclusions South Africans reach, a few realities override all else. However much the ANC has offended many susceptibilities, and alarmed its critics, these realities cannot be wished away. The first is that blacks are governing South Africa. Second, the ANC is the only black party capable, for the present, of leading the government. Third, Mbeki is the only black politician capable, for the present, of leading the ANC. Fourth, black politics have become more, not less, unstable since 1994, and – again for the present – only the ANC has a serious prospect of restabilizing them.

Every judgment of the direction in which South Africa is likely to move after this year's elections will necessarily fall within this fairly rigid paradigm.

# 4 THE POST-APARTHEID ECONOMY: ACHIEVEMENTS, PROBLEMS AND PROSPECTS

*Jesmond Blumenfeld*

## Introduction

When South Africans participated in their first all-race national elections in April 1994, the majority – no matter for which party they voted – confidently expected that the advent of the 'new' South Africa would also mark the beginning of a period of significant economic recovery and expansion after many years of stagnation in output and declining employment. The ensuing five years have brought substantial changes in economic policy as the government has increasingly embraced 'conservative' and 'responsible' stances on micro- and macroeconomic policy issues. Yet, at the second election, the economy is again in recession, there has been relatively little new investment, especially by foreign firms, the number of jobs lost still exceeds the number created, and – despite the processes of transformation, economic empowerment and affirmative action which have benefited a growing number of black households – average income has not risen discernibly.

This chapter sets out to explore the reasons for, and the consequences of, these 'disappointed' expectations, to analyse the successes and failures of economic performance and management over the past five years, and to assess their implications for the future of the post-apartheid economy. The conclusion is twofold: first, that the nature of apartheid's economic legacy was such that the expectations of rapid economic regeneration were excessive and unrealistic; and, second, that, although the post-1994 policy changes have been mostly for the better, much restructuring remains to be done and further uncomfortable policy choices will have to be made if economic performance is to improve substantially over the next five years.

## The new South Africa's economic inheritance

In 1994, many voters arguably had wholly unrealistic expectations that new jobs, houses, pensions, schools and hospitals would somehow flow directly from democracy and political legitimacy. Nevertheless, the general expectation of economic improvement was rational given three acknowledged facts:

- The institutions and policies of apartheid – especially insofar as they had wasted the country's human resources – had severely distorted and damaged South Africa's economic potential and performance.
- Under white minority rule, South Africa had chosen – or as a result of the Second World War and, subsequently, of international sanctions and other external pressures, had been induced – to pursue inward-looking and increasingly isolationist economic policies. Although these policies had long since exhausted most of their potential to generate significant additional benefits by the 1990s, they were still generating substantial additional opportunity costs.
- Confidence in South Africa's economic future had long also been undermined by a pervasive sense of uncertainty about future political and social stability. This was particularly evident in the continuing unwillingness of both domestic and foreign investors to commit resources to long-term productive undertakings.

These three (interrelated) factors had been primarily responsible for serious deterioration in economic performance. The effects were most plainly evident from the early 1980s onwards: in the decade preceding the 1994 election, for example, the average annual growth rate of GDP had been less than one per cent. But economic decline had been discernible for much longer: apart from a brief respite in 1979–81, real income per capita, for example, had fallen almost continuously since 1974, and in 1993 was at its lowest level for 27 years. Similarly, by 1993, gross domestic fixed investment had fallen in all bar five years since 1975.[1]

Yet South Africa's economic resources and potential, including its potential advantages for foreign investment, were considerable. Consequently, the belief that the ending of apartheid, the lifting of international sanctions and reintegration into the global economy constituted not only necessary, but also sufficient, conditions for economic regeneration, was understandable. Moreover, during the processes of transition and negotiation that followed Nelson Mandela's release from prison and the legalization of the ANC and other political organizations in 1990, numerous foreign firms established a presence in South Africa, seemingly presaging a major surge in foreign direct investment (FDI) once the new order was established.

The reality, however, was bound to be rather more complex, for South Africa was entering the post-apartheid era with an economy that was far from being well-suited to the demands and expectations that were to be placed upon it. Undeniably the most advanced economy in Africa, and with the potential to act as the economic 'locomotive' for much of sub-Saharan Africa, it was none the less beset by a crippling skills shortage, extreme degrees of poverty and inequality, serious structural

[1] Except where otherwise indicated, all data in this chapter are derived or computed from the *Quarterly Bulletin* (various issues) or the *Annual Economic Report* (various years) of the South African Reserve Bank.

deficiencies and a host of political and economic uncertainties. It was also about to confront a world increasingly dominated by impersonal market forces that were unlikely to be swayed very far, or for very long, by the view – not uncommonly expressed in some quarters – that South Africa was 'owed a living' by the rest of the world because of the depredations visited on the great mass of its people by apartheid.

## The 'human capital' deficit

The scale of the socio-economic deprivation inflicted by apartheid was indeed vast. The huge backlogs in infrastructural and service provision in housing, education, health, transport and other spheres clearly represented great opportunities for investment and economic development; equally clearly, however, they would also pose major funding burdens for decades to come. In themselves, moreover, the backlogs constituted serious direct obstacles to progress. This was particularly true in the field of 'human capital': deliberate denial of education and training to successive generations of black citizens had left South Africa with grossly inadequate technical, administrative and managerial capacities for confronting its challenges.

## Income and wealth inequalities

Apartheid also bequeathed exceptional degrees of poverty, both absolute and relative. One estimate put the number of people living in absolute poverty in the early 1990s at 46 per cent of the total population; for children, the proportion was 54 per cent; measures of relative poverty suggested that South Africa's income distribution was one of the most unequal in the world. The origins of this poverty lay mainly in the restrictions on the ability of blacks to own land or other property or assets and to acquire income-enhancing skills. One enduring consequence is that the only asset the vast majority of black people have to sell is their labour – but the fact that so many have no job merely perpetuates both the poverty and the inequality.

## The structural adjustment problem

The transition to democracy and the ending of sanctions were only two of many requirements for ensuring South Africa's successful economic regeneration. The long period of isolation had created distortions that were evident in a wide range of structural flaws that could be rectified only through the adoption of appropriate 'structural adjustment' policies. Three of the key indicators were:

- *The lack of international competitiveness of South African manufactures*, as reflected in the low proportion of exports in the total output of manufactured goods, and in the fact that South Africa's share of total manufactured exports from all developing countries plummeted from 11.6 per cent in 1955 to only 1.5 per cent in 1993.[2] The severe price disadvantages faced by manufacturers in international markets were the result, in turn, of the high levels of protection accorded to domestic producers and the low productivity of the manufacturing work force.

- *The 'balance-of-payments constraint'*, which effectively precluded the possibility of achieving sustainably higher rates of economic growth. The constraint had three components. First, domestic production in general, and fixed investment in particular, were highly import-intensive. Second, the majority of export earnings were derived from minerals and raw materials, the demand for which was determined by the state of the world economy, and the prices of which had weakened generally since the 1970s. Third, the rate of domestic savings was low – and declining. Consequently, economic growth was invariably accompanied by a major surge in imports, but not necessarily in exports, often resulting in turn in a current account deficit, and putting the financing of further growth at the mercy of foreign capital inflows.

- *The poor employment-generating capacity of private-sector investment*, reflected in the high capital-intensity (low labour-intensity) of the production techniques adopted by firms. This deficiency had worsened progressively over the decades. Even during the so-called '1960s miracle', when GDP growth rates of up to 5–6 per cent p.a. were achieved, employment growth was substantially slower than the growth in the labour force. By the 1990s, employment absorption had turned negative: the total number of jobs in the non-agricultural 'formal' sector of the economy declined by more than 6 per cent between 1989 and 1993 (in the private sector the decline was more than 10 per cent). 'Formal' employment in agriculture had also declined sharply. In short, unemployment had been rising inexorably for several decades.

Realistically, therefore, it should have been apparent that structural changes of the scope and magnitude required to rectify these problems were going to take rather more than five years to achieve, even under relatively favourable circumstances. Moreover, there was a real possibility of conflict between the policies needed to effect such changes, at least in the short to medium term. This was true especially (though not only) of the twin drives for competitiveness and employment creation. One possibility, however, offered hope of a more optimistic scenario: if long-term foreign capital were to enter South Africa on a sufficiently

[2] See Brian Levy, *How Can South African Manufacturing Efficiently Create Employment? An Analysis of the Impact of Trade and Industrial Policy*, Informal Discussion Papers on Aspects of the Economy of South Africa, No. 1, Southern Africa Department, World Bank, 1992, Table 2.8. See also James Barber's section in Chapter 6.

large scale, this might permit circumvention of these structural impediments, if only temporarily, and so generate enough new resources to make meaningful inroads into the developmental backlogs.

## Political and economic uncertainty

Hopes of such a favourable outcome rested on early resolution of another long-standing economic problem, namely the debilitating effect on real investment of endemic uncertainty about South Africa's political and economic future. In the mid-1990s, there were some helpful portents, including the unprecedented interest being shown by foreign investors, and the world-wide diplomatic suppport for the fledgling democracy. In addition, despite some setbacks along the way, the post-1990 political transition had dramatically reduced the danger of all-out race war. In the process, the ANC – at least as represented by its leadership – had shed much of its socialist rhetoric, including the symbolically important demands for nationalization of the mines, banks and 'monopoly industries'. The ANC also evinced increasing respect for market forces and for the policy orthodoxies that assigned high priorities to 'responsible' monetary and fiscal policies.

Significant though it was, however, fundamental political change was not sufficient in itself to resolve the confidence problem. For potential investors, both foreign and domestic, many unanswered questions still remained, both about the country's long-term political stability and about future macro- and microeconomic policies. The 'political miracle' of relatively peaceful transition may have under-pinned hopes that the daunting challenges to democracy in the post-apartheid era could be overcome, but it did not reduce the magnitude of those challenges. The potential threats to political stability were thus still stark and manifold. No less important were the challenges of economic management, in which the ANC was untried and untested. Would the ANC's conversion to the goals of fiscal and monetary rectitude withstand the political pressures for early delivery of discernible benefits to disadvantaged blacks? Would the (predominantly black) trade unions, which had played such a crucial role in sapping the resistance of the apartheid governments of the 1980s, not make politically irresistible demands for costly employment protection measures and enhanced roles in corporate decision-making? Would exchange controls be maintained or abolished? What would be the ANC's 'real' policies on competition, trade, investment, taxation, privatization, labour-market regulation, affirmative action, mineral rights, wealth redistribution and a host of other issues of direct relevance to the risk and return calculations underlying direct investment decisions?

In short, investment in South Africa still carried many risks, and potential investors were waiting for greater definition of the policy parameters of the post-apartheid era. It was particularly noteworthy that the majority of foreign corporations that established footholds in South Africa in the first half of the 1990s had done so only on a small scale. The intended message seemed clear. Foreign investors were testing the waters: they wanted a base from which they could readily expand if the future started to look more secure; but they also wanted to limit the amount they were putting at risk if it did not.

## The challenge of globalization

During South Africa's exclusion from the global economy, the international 'rules of the game' had changed dramatically. Consequently, the country was seeking reintegration under unfamiliar circumstances. In the sanctions period and, particularly, the decade-long crisis that had been engendered by the unilateral debt moratorium of 1985, South Africa's policy-makers had acquired considerable experience in dealing with foreign capital shortages and their growth-constraining consequences. Now there were hopes and expectations of major, growth-enhancing capital inflows. As the Mexican currency crisis of 1993/4 had demonstrated, however, large capital inflows could be highly volatile and hence also potentially destabilizing. Moreover, the policy context had changed dramatically: under the so-called 'Washington consensus', interventionism (with which South Africa's policy-makers were most familiar) had given way to greater openness to international market forces. But experience elsewhere was showing that the more liberalized environment also appeared to constrain the capacity of national governments, whether in developed or developing countries, to exercise autonomy in economic management. Given the magnitude of the developmental challenges that South Africa was facing, such externally imposed constraints were bound to be problematic.

The South African economy was thus in no fit state to perform all the feats that were about to be asked of it. This was recognized implicitly in the fact that few commentators considered it capable of sustaining growth in excess of 3.5 per cent to 4 per cent p.a. for more than a few years at a time, even assuming sufficient availability of foreign capital. With population still growing at between 2 and 2.5 per cent p.a., this did not suggest that the resources needed to make serious inroads into the apartheid legacy and decisively to reverse the decline in average living standards would soon be forthcoming. This contrasted starkly with Indonesia, Malaysia, South Korea and Thailand – several of the world's other 'emerging market' economies – that had demonstrated the capacity to achieve output growth rates averaging between 7 per cent and 9 per cent p.a. continuously over no less than three decades from 1965 to 1995.[3]

[3] World Bank, *World Development Report*, Oxford University Press (annual, various issues).

## The quest for growth: from the RDP to GEAR to …?

For South Africa, of course, it was entirely appropriate to keep stressing the positive, rather than the negative, aspects of its economic situation. To have done otherwise would have been simply defeatist. And, over and above the obvious point that the peaceful political transition had provided a much more propitious climate for tackling and surmounting the challenges ahead, there were many positive points to stress. Not least was that the growth rate of GDP, which had been negative since late 1989, had risen from 1.3 per cent in 1993 to 2.7 per cent in 1994 and 3.4 per cent in 1995; and that the long-running decline in gross domestic fixed investment had ended in 1994, with a rise of almost 9 per cent, followed by a further 10 per cent increase in 1995.

Moreover, some of the structural adjustment and policy challenges were already being attacked, sometimes with surprising vigour:

- Even before the elections, the ANC, the trade unions and the employers had joined with the 'old' government in negotiating a submission to the General Agreement on Tariffs and Trade (GATT) which committed South Africa to rapid and substantial reductions in industrial protectionism. After the elections, the new government actually reduced some tariffs at a rate faster than the GATT offer required.
- Barely ten months after taking office, the government's liberalizing tendencies seemed to be further confirmed by the abolition of all remaining exchange controls on non-residents via the 'financial rand' dual exchange-rate mechanism.
- The South African Reserve Bank, which had a clear long-term commitment to pursuit of market-oriented monetary policies, was accorded independence from government control.
- There was an impressive display of unity in government over the controversial policy commitment to reduce the relative size of the fiscal deficit: the outgoing administration had allowed the deficit to rise to the dangerously high level of 8.5 per cent of GDP in the fiscal year 1992/3, but by 1995/6 this ratio had been reduced to 6 per cent, with a target of 4 per cent set for 1999/2000.
- It also seemed to augur well that exports, especially of manufactured goods, had been growing apace throughout the political transition period, as sanctions were progressively eroded.
- Even the human capital constraints had been partially relieved by the return to South Africa of many exiles who did have scarce skills; further relief came from international donors, who were offering considerable assistance in training and capacity-building, especially for the public sector.
- Inflation, which also had threatened to get out of hand under the previous government, was on a downward trend. Though still too high relative to South

39

Africa's major trading partners, the inflation rate had fallen from nearly 14 per cent in 1992 to 7.5 per cent in 1996, despite the post-1993 growth upturn.

All these positive developments were reflected in the staunching of the decade-long haemorrhage of capital outflows: despite the need to continue repaying substantial foreign debts, post-election net inflows of foreign capital totalled over R30 billion (£5.5 billion) in the 18 months up to the end of 1995. Increased optimism was mirrored also in share prices and in the rand. From as early as November 1993 to the end of 1994, the all-share price index on the Johannesburg Stock Exchange rose by 40 per cent; and, although the real effective exchange rate of the rand – its inflation-adjusted rate against the currencies of South Africa's major trading partners – fluctuated substantially both before and after the election, its average value during 1994 and 1995 remained relatively steady.

Yet long before the rand suffered its first 'collapse' under the new government in February 1996, it was apparent that the improvements in economic fundamentals, though welcome, fell far short of both expectation and need. The biggest short-comings were in those policy areas where delivery was most directly pertinent to the needs of the impoverished black majority. Despite some successes – most notably in water and electricity supplies – improvements in housing, education and health-care provision were painfully slow to emerge, while the number of jobs destroyed continued to outpace the number newly created. No less disappointing was the continuing absence of any large-scale FDI: the great bulk of the capital inflows were destined for the equity and bond markets, rather than for new fixed investments. There was also increasing doubt about the sustainability of the expansion: despite continuing export growth, even the relatively modest post-election growth threw the current account of the balance of payments into increasing deficit (2.5 per cent of GDP in 1995) and induced the authorities to raise interest rates to restrain the growth rate.

## The RDP

Criticism of this record focused mainly on the Reconstruction and Development Programme (RDP), which started out as the election manifesto of the ANC alliance, but quickly became the centrepiece of the new government's ambitious policy programme for socio-economic transformation. The RDP was presented as 'an integrated, coherent, socio-economic policy framework ... [for mobilizing] people ... [and] resources ... [and for eradicating] the results of apartheid ... [and building] a democratic, non-racial and non-sexist future ... [representing] a vision for the fundamental transformation of South Africa'. It promised 'sustainable' and 'people-driven' programmes that '... [would integrate] growth, development, reconstruction, redistribution and reconciliation into a unified programme ... meet basic needs and open up previously suppressed economic and human potential in urban and rural areas ... [leading to] increased output in all sectors ... [and enhancing] export capacity'.[4] Early versions of the RDP set out 'achievable' targets for the first five years, including the building of more than one million houses; the electrification of a further 2.5 million homes; the redistribution of 30 per cent of land to landless people; and the provision of clean water and sanitation, and access to affordable health care and telecommunications, for 'all' the population. Later versions were more circumspect in setting such specific and ambitious targets.

Initially, the RDP attracted near-universal political support, but lack of progress towards achievement of its targets soon undermined this support. It rapidly became evident that, far from offering an 'integrated and coherent framework' for implementing social and economic policies, the programme in fact suffered from serious political, organizational, procedural and institutional weaknesses, and that its intended role and scope were highly ambiguous as well as ambitious. It was increasingly apparent that a major reason for the failures was the critical shortage of appropriate skills in the public sector. More generally, the RDP, intended perhaps as a device for reconciling the demands of those who recognized the urgent need for policies that would promote rapid economic growth and those who perceived an equally urgent political need for more redistributive policies, proved able to satisfy neither set of protagonists.[5]

By mid-1995, the government had already begun to acknowledge the need for a new policy approach, and particularly for the promotion of economic growth to be accorded a much higher priority (with the goal of redistribution – or 'reconstruction', as it was euphemistically called – implicitly accorded a much lower priority). Such was the political resistance within the ANC alliance to this change in emphasis, however, that it was mid-1996 before a new strategy could be launched, although the RDP was effectively abandoned in March 1996 when the ministry set up to implement it was abolished by President Mandela. In the meantime, the financial markets, tiring (or despairing) of the government's slow pace in defining and implementing more market-friendly and growth-promoting economic policies, had sent the rand into free fall. The real exchange rate fell some 17 per cent between January and December 1996, and was 8.3 per cent lower on average in 1996 than in 1995.

In addition, the domestic business community, acting through the South Africa Foundation, succeeded in defining the two key disputed terrains of economic policy

---

[4] South African Government, *White Paper on Reconstruction and Development*, September 1994, Ch.1.
[5] For evaluations of the RDP, see Jesmond Blumenfeld, 'From Icon to Scapegoat: South Africa's Reconstruction and Development Programme', *Development Policy Review*, Vol. 15, No. 1, March 1997, pp. 65–91, and the references contained therein.

as the fiscal deficit (and the associated issue of privatization) and the labour market. The Foundation argued that, by historical and international standards, and despite the reductions already achieved by the new government, South Africa's budget deficit was still dangerously high. It also argued that the labour market was one of the most rigid in the world, and that these rigidities bore significant responsibility for the escalating scale of unemployment. By failing to reduce the size of the public sector fast enough, by delaying the privatization process (which would attract foreign direct investment, thereby boosting both the foreign exchange reserves and government revenues) and by seeking to increase, rather than decrease, the degree of regulation of the labour market, the government was – in the Foundation's view – sending the wrong signals to international markets and investors. Drastic action on these fronts, as well as on the undisputed issues of the need to reduce crime and promote exports, was necessary if South Africa was to escape from its low-growth trap.[6]

## The GEAR programme[7]

In June 1996, the government finally responded to the growing pressures from economic realities by adopting a new, and more 'market-friendly', macroeconomic strategy. Entitled 'Growth, Employment and Redistribution' (GEAR), the strategy drew heavily on the three themes which have constituted the conventional world-wide policy wisdom of the 1980s and 1990s: improved macroeconomic balance; increased openness to international flows of goods and capital; and greater liberalization of markets. The GEAR programme accordingly committed the government to a range of policy measures which, it predicted, would lead to more rapid and more sustainable economic growth and to the creation of hundreds of thousands of new jobs.[8]

The programme formally set a number of specific targets to be achieved by 2000. These included:

- A GDP growth rate of 6 per cent p.a.
- Creation of more than 1.3 million new 'formal sector' jobs outside agriculture.
- A fiscal deficit/GDP ratio of 3 per cent (compared with the earlier target of 4 per cent).
- A rise in gross domestic savings from 17 per cent of GDP to more than 21 per cent in 2000.

[6] See South Africa Foundation, *Growth for All: An Economic Strategy for South Africa*, Johannesburg, February 1996.
[7] This section draws on parts of Jesmond Blumenfeld, *Assessing South Africa's Growth Strategy*, Briefing Paper No. 49, Royal Institute of International Affairs, London, July 1998.
[8] See Department of Finance, *Growth, Employment and Redistribution: A Macroeconomic Strategy*, Pretoria, June 1996.

- 11 per cent p.a. average growth in real manufactured exports.
- 12 per cent p.a. average growth rate of real investment.

The means by which these goals were to be achieved encompassed a wide range of macro- and microeconomic policies. These included new 'supply-side', cost-reducing investment incentives that eliminated discrimination between domestic and foreign investors; further tariff reductions; maintenance of a stable real exchange rate; a reduction in public-sector employment from 1.2 million to 900,000 employees over three years; budgetary reforms, including a new medium-term framework for budgetary planning; continued relaxation of exchange controls as circumstances permitted; and negotiation of a 'national social agreement' between labour, government and business to ensure that the competitive benefits of the earlier depreciation of the currency were not dissipated by a vicious circle of wage and price increases.

With the possible exception of the 'national social agreement', which seemed to be modelled on continental European practices whose relevance to South Africa was uncertain, these proposed policy mechanisms were unexceptionable and were widely welcomed both at home and abroad. Damaging though the attack on the currency had been, it made sense to seek to exploit the depreciation to boost exports. The commitment to an accelerated reduction in the relative size of the fiscal deficit was particularly striking, although the long-awaited commitment to an active privatization programme was still not forthcoming. Instead, privatization, which was still referred to euphemistically as 'restructuring of state assets', was to be considered only on a case-by-case basis and not as an end in itself. Worryingly – at least from a business perspective – all privatizations would still have to adhere to procedures that had previously been agreed with the trade unions and that were widely interpreted as affording the unions an effective veto over the process.

On the subject of labour-market reforms, GEAR was even more ambiguous. Its proposals covered two themes: productivity enhancement programmes, and the pursuit of 'regulated flexibility'. The latter concept was defined both as 'extending the protection and stability afforded by [the existing] regulatory framework to an increased number of workers', and as allowing for 'flexible collective bargaining structures, variable application of employment standards and voice regulation'. The intended thrust of these reforms was thus unclear.

The adoption of GEAR was of fundamental importance, both politically and economically, in that it signalled not only the government's acceptance of market-imposed criteria for the evaluation of its conduct of macroeconomic policy, but also its eschewal of continuing calls from its radical constituencies for more 'populist' measures. Through its promise of greater macroeconomic stability and more open and less regulated markets, GEAR represented the government's most decisive shift yet away from the dangers of resorting to undisciplined fiscal and monetary policies and increased state intervention. To date, moreoever, GEAR has delivered to a greater or lesser extent on all three of these fronts, the only significant exceptions being privatization and the labour market (see below).

Insofar as it set quantitative targets, however, GEAR's first three years have been singularly unimpressive. Significant progress has been recorded only in respect of the budget deficit and manufactured export growth. Thus, the deficit/GDP ratio declined from 5.1 per cent in 1996/7, to 4.3 per cent in 1997/8 and (probably) 3.7 per cent in 1998/9 (although these represented some slippage in relation to the targets of 4.0 per cent for 1997/8 and 3.5 per cent in 1998/9). As a proportion of total export earnings, manufactured exports more than doubled from 15 per cent in 1990 to 31 per cent in 1997, thereby assisting the ratio of real merchandise exports to GDP to rise from 15.5 per cent in 1990 to almost 23 per cent in 1997. Since 1996, however, growth in manufactured exports appears to have slowed, despite the substantial decline in the real exchange rate during that year. This suggests that the benefits of the ending of sanctions may now have been exhausted and that South Africa's fundamental postwar uncompetitiveness in manufacturing may now have begun to reassert itself.

In output, investment, savings and employment growth, however, performance has been significantly below the GEAR targets:

- GDP grew by 3.1 per cent in 1996, 1.7 per cent in 1997 and was close to zero in 1998, against targets of 3.5 per cent, 2.9 per cent and 3.8 per cent respectively.
- Real private investment growth in 1996, 1997 and 1998 likewise fell well short of its annual targets of more than 9 per cent, achieving only 6.1 per cent, 3 per cent and 2.5 per cent (first half-year) respectively, despite the new incentives.
- Gross domestic savings, far from increasing as a proportion of GDP, fell to a mere 15.2 per cent in 1997, with the ratio apparently still on a downward trend. The consequent need to attract even more foreign savings to finance a higher investment rate will keep real interest rates high and so choke off domestic investment.
- A total of 378,000 new jobs was expected to be created in 1996 and 1997. Instead, non-agricultural private-sector employment continued to fall, bringing the cumulative net job losses between 1989 and 1997 to some 540,000. In agriculture, some estimates suggest the job losses may have been even greater. Meanwhile, employment in the public sector – due to be 'downsized' under GEAR – rose by more than 100,000. The unemployment rate, which reached 37.6 per cent in 1997, is now almost certainly approaching two out of every five people in the economically active population.

Part – but only part – of this disappointing performance can be blamed on 'exogenous' factors, such as the fall in the international gold price (from an average of

$385 in 1994–6 to $331 in 1997 and $295 in 1998), the El Niño weather pheno-menon and, more recently, East Asian 'contagion'. This latest effect manifested itself in May 1998, when the rand plunged 21 per cent against the US dollar within six weeks, forcing the Reserve Bank's repurchase rate up to almost 22 per cent and the prime bank overdraft rate up to the historically high level of 24 per cent. It was South Africa's misfortune that this occurred at exactly the moment when domestic conditions seemed ripe for interest rates – which were already punitively high in real terms – to start falling. The effect was to push the already faltering economy into recession. Although interest rates had begun to move down again by late November, and by mid-March 1999 were again approaching their pre-crisis levels, the outlook for the real economy in 1999 and into 2000 remains bleak. How long the economy stays in recession may depend upon the extent of the political and economic uncertainties surrounding the general election campaign, but even assuming a fair wind, growth in 1999 will still fall well below the population growth rate, bringing another decline in average living standards.

## Whither GEAR?

Unsurprisingly, the evident failure of GEAR to effect economic regeneration, let alone meet most of its targets, threatens to undermine confidence in the programme. Indeed, since it was clear that an early return to sustainable growth was not in prospect even before the onset of Asian contagion, this dismal performance raises the question of whether the GEAR programme was so seriously flawed that it should be fundamentally revised or, perhaps, abandoned. Such a conclusion would not be warranted, however. Although GEAR has had its weaknesses, some of these have stemmed more from failures of implementation than failures of design. And, while there is no guarantee that more determined implementation would now bring greater success, the dangers of deviating too far from the underlying principles of GEAR probably outweigh the risks of persisting with them.

In economic terms, GEAR's weaknesses were both conceptual and practical. First, it should have accorded higher priority to overcoming the 'human capital' deficit. Modern economic theory points to a close link between economic growth and the quality of the labour force; and the apartheid legacy suggests the need for much heavier investment, by both the private and public sectors, in training and education. Second, far too little attention was paid to the need for close coordination between government departments and agencies in the formulation and implemen-tation of policy. Third, the prevarication within government over the speed – and possibly also the principle – of privatization has been damaging, since a more vigorous commitment almost certainly would have had beneficial consequences for the budget balance, and especially for FDI and for policy perceptions.

Perhaps GEAR's most important failing, however, has been in labour-market policy. Investment in South Africa is highly capital-intensive primarily because, in practice, labour is expensive relative to capital. Many variables are relevant here, but – at least in the short term – the only way to reduce the relative price of labour is via lower unskilled wages. The effect, if not the intention, of the government's labour-market policies, however, has been perceived as cost-raising, rather than cost-reducing. Here, even more than with privatization, the government faces an acute political dilemma. The history of discrimination against black workers creates understandable resistance to any erosion of hard-won gains in wage rates and working conditions. These considerations explain the bitterness of recent battles between employers and unions over new legislation covering industrial relations, working conditions and affirmative action. Business considers that government has conceded too much to the unions, and that the consequent increase in labour market rigidities has both inhibited job creation and further damaged investor confidence. In yielding to the unions, the government, for its part, may have been hoping to secure wider acceptance of the push for macro-stability and fiscal rectitude, suggesting a belief in the possibility of a major trade-off which probably did not exist.

Although these issues are ultimately political, rather than economic, in nature, the fact remains that GEAR's failure to deliver in the two policy areas of privatization and labour market reform may do much to account for one of the greatest disappointments of the post-apartheid era, namely the continuing reluctance on the part of foreign companies to undertake direct investments in South Africa. Despite the political transformation, FDI has remained at worryingly low levels, forcing unhealthy – and damaging – reliance on volatile portfolio flows to fund foreign capital needs. An active privatization programme, together with a less regulated labour market, might well have increased the country's attractiveness to FDI. By the same token, the continuing internal dissensions within the ANC alliance over GEAR have compromised the government's credibility over economic management and underpinned lingering concerns that it might yet yield to pressures to reverse significant aspects of its more business-friendly policies.

Given the immensity of the economic challenges, and the magnitude and scope of the structural changes required, it has to be recognized that there are no simple formulae that would guarantee the sustained regeneration of output, let alone employment, growth in South Africa. Nevertheless, the broad thrust of the GEAR programme – towards creating a more stable macroeconomic environment, opening up the economy to international trade and capital flows, and allowing market forces to play a more prominent part in resource allocation decisions – has undoubtedly been a significant step in the right direction. The validity of this point becomes self-evident when the consequences of the old policy regime, with its contrary instincts, are examined.

46

At the same time, persisting with GEAR – and especially with its logical consequences – is also not a risk-free option. It is arguable, for example, that GEAR's thrust could prove damagingly deflationary in present circumstances, particularly if the world economy becomes more fundamentally destabilized. Moreover, following the East Asian crisis, the waters have been muddied by the growing recognition within the wider international policy community that the current orthodoxy may not always lead to the anticipated results. Embarking on a privatization programme, and freeing up the labour market, may not therefore in itself deliver faster growth and more jobs. Much would depend on domestic and external perceptions of the vigour with which foreign capital and the associated technology and commitment were sought, of the government's motives and intentions in reforming the labour market, and of the coherence of the entire economic policy package. It is also arguable that such policies might be doomed to failure in the absence of a more serious attack on the human capital deficit.

Despite these dangers, however, the government should resist the temptation to downgrade the policy objectives encapsulated in GEAR. Having agreed – for better of for worse – to let the markets be the arbiters of appropriate policy, any perceived backtracking on this front could well be a high-risk strategy. In particular, any fiscal relaxation, or other evidence of a return to an unstable or unsustainable macroeconomic stance, would surely be punished mercilessly by the markets. In this respect, as noted above, perceptions, as well as the substance, of policy matter: recent headlines reporting that the US government views the South African government as 'investor unfriendly' underline the point. In short, continuing with the wholehearted – but also carefully integrated – implementation of the GEAR principles at least offers more hope than any known alternative policy package of achieving economic regeneration.[9]

## Conclusion

In 1994, it was widely assumed that if, by 1999, 'insufficient' progress had been made in delivering higher living standards for the impoverished majority, serious political repercussions would ensue. Thus, visions were generated of a second election dominated by a combination of militant trade unionists, angry black township residents and disaffected ANC activists undermining political stability and successfully demanding resort to 'populist' measures which might deliver some short-term gains, but which almost certainly would also compromise some of the required restructuring of the economy. Happily, despite the 'headline' economic

---

[9] See LSE Centre for Research into Economics and Finance in Southern Africa, 'Reflections on South African Political Economy', *Quarterly Review*, No. 2, 1998, pp. 27–36.

failures, and the undoubted distaste among some of the government's constituents for the economic policy shifts that have occurred, no such dissident mass political mobilization has yet materialized; nor does this outcome seem probable in the foreseeable future. To this extent, South Africa still has the opportunity to root out the adverse structural consequences of apartheid's economic legacy and to create an enabling environment for renewed and sustainable output and employment growth. On the evidence of the first five years, however, much work still remains to be done.

# 5 CIVIL SOCIETY

## A: GOOD GOVERNANCE AND ACCOUNTABILITY
### *Heather Deegan*

Popular acceptance of democracy derives from the performance of the government, not only in the socio-economic sphere but also in terms of its capacity to maintain order, to govern with probity and transparency, to uphold the rule of law and to respect and preserve democratic behaviour. Under the 1996 constitution a comprehensive framework for the practice of good governance has been established which repeatedly affirms the need for accountable, open and effective government. However, although the final constitution holds all members of the cabinet accountable collectively and individually to parliament, it was not signed into law until December 1996. When the 1994 elections took place, the temporary, transitional constitution was still in effect and that document did not provide clear or substantive definitions of legislative authority. During the past five years, then, parliament has evolved in both procedural and institutional senses.

## Parliament

The new constitution established a bicameral structure, the National Assembly and a second chamber, the National Council of Provinces, which was intended to provide greater powers to the provinces in the legislative process and improve levels of accountability. The National Council of Provinces was introduced in February 1997 and it is generally accepted that it has yet to develop its role fully, whereas the performance of the National Assembly has received rather a mixed assessment. On the one hand, and nothwithstanding the difficulties of the transition – inexperienced MPs, fundamental changes in procedures and restricted resources – parliament has performed well in terms of the quantity of laws it has passed: 108 bills per session over the first three parliamentary sessions. Equally, in the early period the new legislators were keen to monitor officials and ministers. On the other hand, more recently there appears to have been some drift, particularly over key pieces of legislation; for example, the government's major economic policy, the GEAR programme, was largely an executive decision with very little input by parliament.

A variety of parliamentary portfolio and select committees, empowered to initiate legislation, have been introduced and expanded in order to enhance accountability. They are open to the public and all committees may summon people to give evidence or provide documentation. These innovations should be seen as major strides towards greater transparency but they have also created problems of their own: a greatly expanded workload and an increased need for more intensive research and better resources. Inevitably, the committees have tended to be constrained by institutional and procedural demands. There are now around 50 committees (previously there were 13), and with the passing of the final constitution much time has been spent in actually adapting to new parliamentary rules. This situation has led to uncertainty among MPs about their areas of responsibility and party allocation of seats within the new committees. Additionally, when these factors are combined with legislative time constraints, budgetary limitations and administrative shortages, their ability to scrutinize government activities obviously becomes compromised.

Representation in both Houses is dominated by the ANC, which thus inevitably has extensive influence over the legislatures. In a tight and disciplined party system ANC MPs are not encouraged to criticize their own ministers. Equally, the fact that legislators represent no electoral constituency and, therefore, have no direct accountability to the voters creates a political environment in which MPs are further locked into dependence upon their respective parties. Inevitably, this is one of the drawbacks of the electoral proportional representative list system. Clearly, during the past five years parliament has experienced fundamental procedural changes that still have to be managed, comprehended and fully implemented. Since 1995 a task team, set up by Thabo Mbeki, has been working on an Open Democracy Bill. This policy document is supposed to put flesh on the bones of the constitutional right of individual access to information in the public and private spheres. The process has been hesitant, with at least four versions of the bill being presented since 1996, and the issue is yet to be fully resolved. One of the central difficulties is that of finding a correct balance between giving effect to the openness envisaged by the constitution and the need for government to operate effectively. Government departments began to feel uneasy about the notion of holding their planning and policy-making meetings in public. Although since 1994 there has been much talk of governance being open to the people in order that they may be carried along with the process of democratic change, South Africa is finding that, as in most liberal democracies, 'open government' is exceptionally difficult to implement without severely compromising the necessary confidentiality of cabinet decision-making. Executive accountability usually rests within parliamentary chambers but this requires political will and responsibility from both government and opposition parties. With less than half the electorate feeling they can trust national government and parliament, no politician should feel over-complacent.

## Local government

Local government has been something of a Cinderella: burdened with onerous tasks and hampered by a lack of resources, it has come to be regarded as both ineffective and inefficient. There are currently 840 municipalities and around 12,000 councillors. The 1995/96 local elections were regulated by temporary legislation, the Local Government Transition Act 1993, and as the electoral turnout was low (38 per cent of the total electorate), questions about public awareness and interest were raised from the start. Until 1995 most rural areas had never had local government structures, while in the metropolitan areas general responses to local government were partly conditioned by the policies of resistance and boycott developed under the apartheid regime. So from the beginning there were profound problems and inevitably local government consistently receives the worst ratings by citizens in terms of performance, trust and corruption.

One of the central difficulties is the issue of revenue raising. Although resources are allocated to local authorities from provincial government, some revenue has to be raised by the municipalities themselves. A major national campaign (Masakane Campaign) was established to educate the population that services such as water, electricity, sanitation etc. had to be paid for by local indigenous communities. With around 65 per cent of the people in townships not paying for their services, the task of building a community culture of payment was immense. Some urban authorities started instalment rates system accounts, into which local constituents paid whatever they could afford, but in general the campaign has largely failed and resulted in rate and rent strikes which have further exacerbated community relations. Caught in a vicious cycle of so-called 'non-compliance' or 'the culture of entitlement', in which communities refuse to pay for services until after they have been received and authorities cannot provide services until rates have been paid, local government has reached a critical point.

Although, potentially, local government can be successful, if it is able to deliver basic services it needs improved institutional capacity, properly trained staff, effective systems of collecting and monitoring of payments, skilled administration, appropriate funding and reformed popular attitudes towards service provision. In a sense, the government's promotion of the short-lived Reconstruction and Development Programme which aimed at 'meeting the basic needs of the people' raised expectations of the performance of local government which it could never fulfil. Under the 1996 constitution, however, local government is a distinct sphere of government vested with executive and legislative powers and in future should not be compromised by other spheres of government.

## Civil society/NGOs

One of the most important elements in promoting greater accountability is the role played by civil society in mediating between government and the wider community. Civil society, expressed through the actions of pressure groups, business associations, trade unions, voluntary societies, women's organizations, churches, etc., provides channels for public expression. South Africa has enjoyed a strong civic federation built upon township resistance movements, as well as around 54,000 non-governmental organizations (NGOs), which formerly raised R1 billion from external funding. In fact, one of the notable achievements of the extra-parliamentary opposition to apartheid was the mushrooming of NGOs and the strengthening of civil society. However, once the 1994 elections took place and the government assumed authority, foreign monies dried up and many NGO leaders entered politics, standing in national, provincial and local elections on ANC platforms. Civil society has changed dramatically and is undergoing a transitional crisis. One difficulty in the new political climate is the blurring of the relationship between civil society and party politics. Ideally, a distinction should be drawn between civic/interest groups and government, yet often there is an overlap between collective interests and political representation. The tripartite alliance between the ANC, COSATU and the South African Communist Party is a case in point. Undue pressure placed upon government from one section of civil society runs the risk of imbalance in policy-making decisions. Moreover, a close funding relationship between the government and NGOs potentially undermines the latter's independence, freedom and flexibility. Many NGOs now compete for contracts from government and are jokingly referred to as 'gongos' (a government NGO) because they uncritically follow the official line.

The South African National Civic Organization (SANCO), which has 900 affiliates and which orchestrated the internal resistance to apartheid, is also in difficulties. In the past, it has shown strident opposition to the government particularly in 1996, when it organized strikes and demonstrations against local government measures to gain payment for rates/services. Seeing itself as independently defending grassroot interests, SANCO has a relationship with the ANC that is at times too close to be comfortable or objective. Partially co-opted into the government's National Economic Development and Labour Council (NEDLAC), and therefore part of the decision-making coterie, many of its affiliated civic organizations are ANC-dominated and in the 1995 local elections it officially backed ANC candidates. There is a lack of clarity about SANCO's role and a big question-mark over its future as a collective organization with its attendant financial problems and internal in-fighting. Clearly, if it wishes to be effective in holding government to account and in representing the very real needs of the poor, it must first distance itself from the ANC and act coherently and consistently.

## Popular demands of government

Issues identified as priorities by the general population tend to reflect racial anxieties: job creation is seen as the most important problem by 72 per cent of black South Africans and 60 per cent of the coloured community, while criminal violence causes most concern among 80 per cent of white and 90 per cent of Indian communities.[1] However, on a scale of priorities all racial groups, in both urban and rural areas, identify housing and education as significant problems. In essence, then, core issues – job creation, crime, housing and education – preoccupy all races but to varying degrees. No government could feasibly remedy the profound injustices of the apart-heid system in one term of office, or perhaps even indeed in one generation, but certain attitudes are changing, particularly towards political violence. Since 1994 the government has supported a comprehensive strategy to help prevent politically motivated killings, and national opinion ratings have reflected a softening in the general population's attitudes towards political tolerance.[2]

Over the past few years public opinion surveys have been conducted in order to assess general popular attitudes and expectations of government. According to national polls, 41 per cent of respondents are satisfied with democracy and 59 per cent are unsatisfied. This suggests that it may be too early to rely upon the idea of a strong societal democratic political culture. This is especially true if we consider the responses to the question posed: 'What if democracy does not work?' Only 47 per cent considered democracy to be always best, while 43 per cent favoured a strong, non-elected leader and 10 per cent did not know.[3] These replies raise questions about legitimacy and governance and indicate that popular support for liberal democratic norms must not yet be taken for granted.

## Corruption and accountability

One worrying trend is the public perception of corruption in public office. In 1997, 50 per cent of voters believed that officials in government departments were engaged in corruption and illegally using public monies for their own benefit or

[1] IDASA Public Opinion Service Report, No. 5, July 1998.
[2] Ibid., No. 8, May 1996.
[3] Ibid., No. 3, February 1996.

taking bribes; 44 per cent believed this was the case in both local councils and provincial government; and 41 per cent thought it was true of national parliament. Only the office of the president received the relatively lower rating of 25 per cent.[4] If there is a lack of popular belief in the probity of public office the government must demonstrate that it will root out any misdemeanours or corrupt practices irrespective of party political affinities. Otherwise, a climate of endemic corruption will set in and gradually erode the democratic base of society. In a sense the accountability of the government depends on the wider population gaining greater access to information. In this respect a vigilant media is shining a light into government/bureaucratic activity and is prepared to discuss sensitive and controversial issues. The Public Protector and the Public Service Commission are also important agencies in establishing codes of conduct.

## Conclusion

So can there be good governance in South Africa? Yes, if the next administration is prepared to bring courage, probity and determination to the heart of public office. Accountable government, however, may make greater demands of politicians and political parties. It is crucially necessary for the ANC, as the dominant political force within the country, to demonstrate that it is completely scrupulous in its democratic instincts, responses and handling of criticism and opposition. Unlike Nelson Mandela in 1994, Thabo Mbeki will lead a country in which the constitutional framework provides for far greater levels of transparency within all branches of government. This will present great challenges to both government and opposition and will require political commitment and energy. The legitimacy and viability of oppositionist parties and groups are also central to the issues of both governance and accountability, but what might the future hold? If South Africa increasingly develops, improves educational opportunities, expands and differentiates its economy, and continues to expose its population to technological change and mass communications, political parties and civic organizations will change and reconfigure themselves in order to fulfil a wider range of popular interests and demands. In the final analysis, good government is only truly accountable when it runs in parallel with potent, responsible and legitimate opposition together with an informed plural civil society.

[4] Ibid., No. 3, February 1998.

54

# Khehla Shubane

## The ANC and centralist tendencies

After the second democratic elections, the political environment in South Africa is expected to be very different. Not only will there be a new president but the notion of a government of national unity will no longer be a constitutional requirement.

One issue in particular has attracted a fair amount of attention: the ANC administration may effect far-reaching changes to existing relations between central and provincial governments. The attention given to this issue follows suggestions by the ANC that it will seek a two-thirds majority in the election in order to speed up the transformation which, in its view, has been blocked by parties historically representing white constituencies. Opposition parties are so weak in South Africa, however, that they have not really prevented the ANC, with its comfortable parliamentary majority, from introducing any policies it desired. Besides, the ANC has not made it clear which of the provisions of the constitution it would alter were it to gain a two-thirds majority.

According to survey evidence, such a majority will be very difficult for the ANC to attain; and, more important, it may be in the interest of the party not to achieve it. In dealing with its radical supporters, the ANC has argued until now that it needs to work with other parties in crafting policy. With that majority it would have to find other reasons to convince its left-wing supporters why certain market-friendly policies should not be adopted.

So keen is the ANC to increase its electoral support that it has not hidden its disappointment in not winning the provinces of KwaZulu-Natal and the Western Cape (the latter is now held by the New National Party), and is working hard to correct what it views as a historical wrong.

It is generally feared that the ANC, with its long history of centralism and opposition to federalism, will diminish the still limited autonomy which provinces have enjoyed until now. The ANC refuses to accept that South Africa should be considered a federal state even though federal features underpin the constitution. Since coming to power, the central government has not surrendered power to the provinces; instead, ministers have often used their powers to maintain certain norms and standards across provinces and to consolidate power at the centre.

Admittedly, however, the provinces have not shown innovation in extending the powers that they can exercise. Although policing powers reside at central government level, for instance, local monitoring and oversight powers are devolved to individual provinces. This potentially extensive power has not been exploited by any province to increase the accountability of police officials to provincial parliaments and thus to claw back a degree of control over policing from central government.

Although the provinces have enjoyed a degree of autonomy, the ANC has continued to lean in the direction of greater centralization of power. The appointment of provincial premiers by the National Executive Committee (NEC) of the ANC exemplifies this trend. This will result in premiers becoming answerable to the NEC rather than the party structures in the provinces. The ANC's aim of ending infighting for leadership positions among its members in provinces will not be achieved by centralizing power.

The political party machinery, at both central and provincial level, has been used more frequently to achieve centralist goals. While the ANC governs a country with relatively autonomous tiers of government, it functions virtually as a unitary party where provincial structures are viewed more as branches than as autonomous parts of a federation. This gives ANC national leaders considerable power to impose uniformity within the entire organization.

In addition a lack of expertise in performing numerous functions at a provincial level bolsters the centralist impulses preferred by the national leadership. In the process of law-making, for example, provinces have been given a say in this process by the constitution, but they hardly use these powers because they cannot meet the requirements set out in the constitution. The National Council of Provinces (NCOP), to which all provinces send an equal number of delegates, was created to ensure that provinces participate in the making of national legislation. For this to happen provinces must mandate their delegates to the NCOP so that their participation in the national process derives from positions which have been canvassed within the provinces themselves. Often, however, provincial delegates debate issues in the NCOP without first obtaining a mandate from their legislatures. Law-making has been proceeding under severe time pressures imposed by the national parliament. It has often been difficult to coordinate this with the provincial legislatures. The latter should preferably meet once the law has been passed by the national assembly and before it goes to the NCOP, which functions as a second chamber of parliament. Any law passed by the national assembly has been through the committee stage where parties have had a say in shaping it. If it then goes through the same process in provincial legislatures parties will divide in exactly the same way over contentious issues as they did when the matter was debated in the national assembly. Herein lies the significance of the unitary nature of the ANC, whose internal party discipline can be used to ensure that provincial party structures do not frustrate what it has already agreed to at the national level.

Often, however, provincial legislative processes cannot meet the short time-frames of the national parliament, and delegates at the NCOP take their cue from their parties rather than their legislatures.

There remain severe difficulties in the way of greater provincial autonomy. One crucial impediment is the almost total lack of an independent revenue base. Most taxes are derived nationally and thus accrue to central government, which consequently decides how these revenues are spent. For example, pensions are determined and now dispensed by the national government, which also established the quantum of housing subsidies to the very poor and pupil-teacher ratios in schools. Even though intergovernmental fiscal relations are geared towards ensuring that all tiers of government receive their fair share of nationally derived revenues, the provinces do not have discretion over their entire allocation.

Politically, an ANC-led central government may be uncertain about what some provinces would do with all the powers they demand. Two of the nine provinces are governed by parties other than the ANC. Until recently the ANC was locked in a bitter conflict with the IFP and could not be expected to support the granting of greater powers to its political competitor. A similar political problem existed with regard to the NNP which governed the Western Cape. However, the attitude of the ANC may now be changing.

## Party electoral support

In the past two years there have been quarterly surveys on public political preferences, and although some were conducted far too early for any useful conclusions about the level of electoral support for any party, their predictions have been consistent over time and may indicate the overall levels of support. All these surveys show that many people have not decided which party they intend voting for or will not cast a vote at all. The figure in this latter category has varied between 12 and 20 per cent – not too large by international standards but large for a country in which democracy is new. However, many people in these categories are likely to decide to vote nearer the elections.

Surveys have consistently indicated that neither the ANC nor any other party has succeeded in attracting 50 per cent of electoral support in the Western Cape or KwaZulu-Natal. Surprisingly, however, polls suggest that the ANC's share of the vote in these provinces has overtaken that of its main rivals.

Survey evidence also suggest that the Northern Cape and Gauteng, both of which are currently governed by the ANC, may not produce a majority government in the next elections. Again, no single party seems capable of generating a level of support which will enable it to govern alone.

This raises the potential for coalition governments in four of the nine provinces. In an age when ideology has played a decreasing role in marking differences among parties, it is unlikely to be critical; practical requirement will be far more important.

Thus, in the Western Cape, a likely post-election scenario is that the NNP and the

DP will cooperate to prevent an ANC government. Such a coalition is already a reality and appears to be working well. But in the Northern Cape, where the ANC won the last election by a narrow margin, the party will continue its current cooperation with the DP to produce a majority government, since both parties will be keen to prevent an NP government there. In KwaZulu-Natal the ANC and the IFP are likely to cooperate in government; both parties have been involved in negotiations for some time. It is generally thought that these discussion are intended to pave the way for cooperation at the national as well as provincial level of government.

One factor which might wreck the growing rapport between the IFP and the ANC is the evolving relationship between the ANC and the UDM, a new political party in the province. In the midlands area the two parties have been involved in bitter conflict which has resulted in fatalities. The assassination of the KwaZulu-Natal leader of the UDM, Sifiso Nkabinde, may trigger more violence in the province. The relationship between the ANC and the IFP hinges in part on this question.

It is much more difficult to predict what will happen in Gauteng. In part this results from the ANC's difficulty in accepting that it may fail to attract 50 per cent of the vote and be able to form a government on its own, despite the survey evidence. Relations among parties in the province have also been very caustic and this will make for a difficult process of cooperation should this be necessary.

Given also that the ANC is unlikely to obtain a two-thirds majority in the national elections, it becomes clear that the constitution is unlikely to be changed at all. Thus, the transformation will to have to be effected within the prevailing political constraints. After the elections, the policy environment for the ANC will remain the same and it will still have to continue to cooperate with other parties. When it comes to introducing policy measures this cooperation will be limited because opposition parties will remain as weak as they are now. The real limitation on the ANC's power is its deep desire to gain acceptability with international investors and multilateral institutions. So determined is it to maintain these relationships that it has defended GEAR, a document which sets out the party's conservative macroeconomic views, even though significant groups which support the ANC do not agree with GEAR's underlying assumptions.

It is possible that in the future the provinces will claim more powers from central government. Provincial policy-makers have learnt much over recent years and may now feel more confident in their competence. This growing confidence is certain to increase differences among the provinces too, and this will lead weaker provinces to seek to emulate their stronger counterparts. The power and autonomy of provincial governments are also likely to be enhanced by the fact that the ANC may either lose power in several provinces or be forced to share power. Such provinces will not be malleable to central government policy prescriptions.

Holding separate elections (on the same day as national balloting) for provincial governments also has the potential to enhance provincial autonomy. In a rather limited way provincial parties have been forced to focus on the needs of their electorates. The political dynamics within provinces have imposed certain limitations as well as opening up possibilities which do not relate solely to the needs of the party at a national level. The ANC provides an apt example in this respect; it maintains a lukewarm relationship with the DP at a national level, cooperates with it in the Northern Cape and is in fierce competition with it in Gauteng.

Impulses towards greater centralization which are evident at a national level within the ANC will have to contend with numerous countervailing forces both within and outside the party. Some of these forces are induced by political imperatives and others by constitutional realities. Greater centralization can be achieved only if the ANC wins elections in all the provinces as well as at a national level. This looks singularly unlikely. Moreover, provincial identities which have developed within the ANC itself would have to be eradicated; this too would take time to achieve. Thus relationships between the provinces and the national government will be affected by tensions which have already had an impact, as well as by a number of complex political, social and economic variables.

One area which provinces have not explored with any vigour is the extent to which they can enhance their powers by enhancing efficiency. There is no reason why any policy should be implemented in exactly the same way in all the provinces. Gauteng has used its right to collect taxes locally – a sum amounting to R1 billion. For a province with a total annual budget of some R14 billion, any increase in the amount due to increased efficiency would be significant and would vastly increase the areas over which the province could exercise budgetary discretion. While the ability of many provinces to levy taxes is limited by their very narrow tax bases, for others revenue flows the size of Gauteng's are not impossible, and would lead to substantial benefits in terms of autonomy.

## C: DEMOCRACY AND STABILITY IN THE NEW SOUTH AFRICA: HUMAN RIGHTS WITH SPECIAL REFERENCE TO THE TRC

### *Merle Lipton*

A dilemma confronting the framers of South Africa's new constitution was whether to deal with the country's painful past by responding to the demands for retribution of many victims and critics of the apartheid regime, or whether to cultivate amnesia about the past in the interests of future political stability. The outcome was a compromise – an agreement to grant conditional amnesty to the perpetrators of gross human rights violations, while setting up a Truth and Reconciliation Commission (TRC) to provide some public acknowledgment and reparation for the victims of gross abuses.

The provision of amnesty was (and continues to be) controversial. But, as Archbishop Desmond Tutu, chairman of the TRC, explained:

> The Amnesty clause made South Africa's 1994 election possible. It was the final clause inserted [into the 1993 Interim Constitution] in the early hours of the morning after an exhausting night of negotiating. It was only when that clause was put in that the *boere* signed the negotiations, opening the door to our election. (Krog, p. 23)

In May 1995, South Africa's newly elected National Assembly passed the 'Promotion of National Unity and Reconciliation Act'. This set up the TRC with the mandate to establish as complete a picture as possible of the causes, nature and extent of the gross violations of human rights committed under apartheid from March 1960 to December 1993 (later extended to May 1994) by conducting investigations and holding hearings. The 17-member commission was to consist of three committees. *The Human Rights Violations Committee* was to investigate gross violations of human rights and had extensive powers to gather documentary evidence and compel the attendance of witnesses. *The Reparation and Rehabilitation Committee* was to formulate a reparation policy and restore and rehabilitate the lives of victims and survivors of violations. *The Amnesty Committee* would have the power to grant amnesties on condition that the applicant made a full disclosure of the facts; that the motivation of the offence was political; and that there was 'proportionality' between the illegal act committed and the political objective. An unusual feature of South Africa's truth commission was that, in addition to its hearings on gross human rights violations (defined as killing, abduction, torture or severe ill-treatment), it also held special 'sectoral' hearings on the conduct of the media, medical and legal professions and business. But it was the hearings on human rights

60

violations that formed the major part of the TRC's work and captured public attention.

There was opposition to the establishment of the TRC. Among the doubters were Nelson Mandela and F.W. de Klerk, both of whom feared that investigating the past, and holding the hearings in public, would stir up hostilities and resentments, thus impeding, rather than promoting, reconciliation (Adam, 1998). There was opposition to the amnesty provisions on the grounds that justice required the prosecution of perpetrators of human rights abuses. Steve Biko's family and others challenged the constitutionality of the amnesty provision – a legal challenge that was rejected by the new Constitutional Court (Lipton, 1998). Others argued that the TRC's 'narrow and legalistic' terms of reference would result in a limited focus on a small group of victims and perpetrators of gross abuses, such as torture and murder, while ignoring both the much larger group of victims and beneficiaries of the whole apartheid system (Mamdani, 1996). The domination of the TRC by commissioners sympathetic to the ANC led its political rivals, especially the NP and Inkatha, to fear that the hearings would turn into a witchhunt against them and a rubber stamp of the ANC's views.

Later, during the couple of years spanning the TRC's work, there was criticism of its rushed proceedings and its focus on a small number of high-profile national cases, to the neglect of the large number of acute conflicts at local level within black communities. The TRC was denounced by the white right as the 'Crying and Lying Commission' which accepted untested allegations and was out to discredit Afrikaners. It was also criticized by some NGOs and human rights activists who felt they had been ignored and sidelined by the Commission and disliked the 'gravy train' aspects of its conduct, as the Commissioners voted themselves big pay rises and other perks. However, many of these criticisms of the TRC were stilled, or at least reduced, by its public hearings, and by the publication of its report.

## The TRC's hearings and findings

The TRC began its public proceedings in April 1996. Over 21,000 statements were received from victims, 2,000 of these in open public hearings, which were widely reported and broadcast on TV and radio. The TRC also received almost 8,000 applications for amnesty from perpetrators. The TRC's hearings had a significant impact on public opinion, shocking many whites into the acknowledgment that gross abuses, including torture and murder, were inflicted on many blacks (and on some white opponents of the government) by agents of the apartheid regime. However, many whites denied thay had known what was happening. This included former President de Klerk, who testified that, while his government had authorized unconventional methods against its opponents, these did not include aberrations such as murder and torture, which were due to 'the bad judgment, over-zealousness and negligence' of individual state agents (Krog, pp. 105, 126). Former President Botha represented the unrepentant wing of white opinion, insisting he had nothing to apologize for and refusing to testify before the TRC (Krog, p. 267).

The hearings also exposed some of the deep conflicts and divisions within black society – divisions which were often deliberately widened by the apartheid government. These conflicts were dramatically illustrated during the sessions on the Winnie Mandela case and in the cases involving necklacing and other violent actions against alleged collaborators. The horrific atrocities and tragic cases discussed at the hearings revealed the complexity of social relationships and the difficulty of judging the behaviour of individuals caught in difficult and dangerous political situations. Few people now publicly justify the evils involved in the attempt to enforce apartheid, or the morality of opposing it, but it was evident that most whites had readily closed their eyes to these appalling effects, while most blacks had kept their heads down and tried to get on with their own lives.

The TRC's report was presented to President Mandela in October 1998. The Commissioners drew attention to some unique features of South Africa's attempt to come to terms with its painful past. First, the investigation was not limited to violations committed by agents of the former apartheid regime, but also covered the conduct of the government's political opponents. This was in keeping with the spirit of promoting reconciliation and with the intention of avoiding such abuses in the future and of establishing a human rights culture. Second, the TRC stressed the important role played by South Africa's unusual 'conditional amnesty' process in precipitating confessions and information from security and military personnel, who would otherwise have had little incentive to provide information about their misdeeds.

The starting point of the TRC's report was the UN declaration that apartheid was a crime against humanity and that opposition to it was morally and politically justified. The report argued that the main responsibility for the extensive violations of human rights that occurred thus rested with the apartheid government and with those, such as Inkatha, who had colluded with it in committing atrocities. However, the report maintained that the fact that the government's opponents were fighting a 'just war' did not justify the perpetration of abuses by the ANC and PAC against civilians and against some of their own members in their military and training camps.

The report commended the willingness of ANC leaders, such as Thabo Mbeki and Mac Maharaj, to testify before the Commission, and the willingness of the ANC leadership to take collective responsibility for the human rights violations of its membership and to conduct their own inquiries into the excesses at their Quatro and other camps. This contrasted with the unwillingness of NP leaders to acknowledge their responsibility – which the TRC saw as a missed opportunity to contribute towards reconciliation. The TRC also regretted the refusal of Inkatha to testify and to seek amnesty. This refusal could prove costly for many of its members, who would not now be eligible for the reparations that were due to be paid to those victims of gross abuses whose claims had been established before the Commission. The report criticized both the liberation movements and Inkatha for their high levels of political intolerance, which had provided a milieu within which violence could readily be stimulated by 'third force' activities. The TRC's report also highlighted the failure of influential members of society, such as lawyers, doctors and business people, who were, at best, guilty of acts of omission in not doing enough to oppose apartheid and who thereby contributed to the 'culture of impunity' which facilitated the violations of human rights.

## Reactions to the TRC's report

The publication of the TRC's 3,500-page report in October 1998 evoked reactions which illuminated some of the fault-lines within South African society. Initially, there were angry reactions both from de Klerk, who secured a court order to remove some critical references to his role, and from Mbeki and others in the ANC. The latter tried to halt publication on the grounds that the TRC's finding that the ANC was guilty of human rights abuses failed to recognize that they were fighting a just war and that their actions could not be equated with those of the apartheid government. These objections were, however, swiftly stilled by President Mandela, who said they were over-reactions based on a hasty reading of the summary of the findings and insisted on publication of the full report.

The attacks from these opposing quarters enhanced the credibility of the TRC, making it clear that it was not an ANC rubber stamp. It also served to rally round the NGOs and human rights activists, who had become increasingly critical of the Commission's flaws and shortcomings, but now felt that these were outweighed by its basic integrity and goodwill. The conflicting reactions within the ANC highlighted significant differences between the approach of Mbeki and of Mandela and Tutu. For Tutu and Mandela reconciliation was the first step – the beginning of the process of transforming society. But Mbeki viewed reconciliation as the end of a process which required reparation for the victims of apartheid. According to Mbeki: 'real reconciliation cannot be achieved without a thorough transformation and democratization process' (Krog, pp. 58, 110).

The TRC's report highlights a number of issues that will have to be dealt with by the parliament and government elected in mid-1999. First is the question of amnesty. The Amnesty Committee is still sifting through the thousands of applications that remain to be considered. There have been calls for a general amnesty so as to draw a line under South Africa's painful past. But the TRC's report urged that prosecutions of those who had not applied for amnesty should now proceed. A number of state prosecutors, as well as victims and their families, are already planning criminal and civil proceedings against perpetrators who failed to apply for amnesty.

Second is the issue of reparations. There is resentment that so little has been done for the victim of abuse, while many perpetrators have already been amnestied. The TRC recommended a reparation and rehabilitation programme for the victims, urging the government to make available an interim payment of R100 million for the estimated 30,000 victims, plus a further sum of R3 billion to be paid to them over six years.

The third, longer-term issue is that of reconciliation. The TRC's report argues that this will require far-reaching redistribution to close the still 'intolerable gap' between rich and poor in South Africa. The report urged the establishment of a special fund for the training, empowerment and creation of opportunities for the disadvantaged, as well as appropriate economic policies such as wealth taxes. It urged the private sector to actively support the government in working for these aims.

Other recommendations made in the TRC's report include the call for a National Summit on Reconciliation, representing all sectors of South African society, to be held at the end of 1999; an extensive education programme to inform South Africans about the past and to nurture a strong human rights culture; the reform of institutions such as the judiciary and the police; and a commitment never again to enact legislation indemnifying the police and other security agencies against human rights abuses.

The TRC made considerable progress in exposing and confirming the truth about many horrific deeds in South Africa's past. But most observers deny that it has achieved much reconciliation – at least in the short term. In the longer term, the exposure of some of the truth about the effects of apartheid may provide a firmer basis for a new national identity within a shared society. However, reconciliation will clearly not be simply and quickly secured, especially given the lack of contrition among the many whites who are still 'in denial' over their responsibility for the apartheid past. Meanwhile, the TRC's proceedings and findings have provided a mirror image of South African society, revealing the still serious rifts between whites and blacks, and among blacks, as well as the commitment to reduce conflict and promote reconciliation. The healing of apartheid's wounds will be influenced both by the continuing willingness of blacks to forgive and of whites to reduce racism and black poverty.

# References

Adam, Heribert, 'Trading Justice for Truth', *World Today*, January 1998.

Hamber, Brandon and Steve Kibble, *From Truth to Transformation: South Africa's Truth & Reconciliation Commission* (CIIR, 1999).

Krog, Antjie, *Country of My Skull* (Random House, 1998).

Lipton, Merle, 'Evaluating South Africa's Truth and Reconciliation Commission' (Conference report, Centre for Southern African Studies, Sussex University, 1998).

Mamdani, Mahmoud, 'Reconciliation without Justice', in *Southern African Review of Books*, November/December 1996.

*Report of Truth & Reconciliation Commission*, website: //www.truth.org.za

# 6 FOREIGN POLICY

## A: FOREIGN POLICY AND THE AFRICAN RENAISSANCE
### Graham Evans

## Introduction

Foreign affairs are unlikely to figure prominently in South Africa's second all-inclusive elections in 1999. These elections will be won or lost on the Government of National Unity's record and manifesto pledges on economic, social and welfare issues. As has been described in earlier chapters, five years after the 'miracle' of the transition the issues that concern a largely impoverished and somewhat disillusioned electorate exercising democratic rights for only the second time in their turbulent history are decidedly domestic. Jobs, housing, public utilities, education, health, crime – these are the matters that South Africans care about now that the high political questions of state legitimacy and constitution-making have been resolved. In this sense at least, South Africa is now a normal state; that is, one where bread-and-butter survival issues take priority over niceties associated with rival political theories.

Nevertheless, South Africa's international relations will have a direct bearing on the ability of Pretoria's second post-apartheid administration to deliver its electoral pledges. The customary distinction drawn by political analysts between international and domestic policy may still hold true for electoral politics, but in every other respect it is misleading. Most issue-areas are now 'intermestic'.[1] That is, issues that dominate political discourse in pluralistic political communities tend to bring together actors from both 'international' and 'domestic' contexts. This is true in terms both of their social impact and of the decision-making framework within which they are handled. Trade, commerce, fiscal stability, investment policy, drugs, immigration are obvious examples of intermestic issues. In fact, the relentless

[1] This term was coined by B. Manning in an article in *Foreign Affairs*, Vol. 55, No. 2, 1977, pp. 306–25. For an elaboration of its meaning beyond the context of US foreign policy, see G. Evans and J. Newnham, *The Penguin Dictionary of International Relations* (Harmondsworth: Penguin Books, 1998), p. 258.

process of globalization and complex interdependence during the post-Cold War period means that virtually every aspect of state policy in open, closed, developed and developing societies now has intermestic characteristics.

Global economic enmeshing has proceeded at such a pace that what goes on outside the territorial boundaries of the state often conditions what can be achieved within them. Further, the irrelevance of sovereignty as a practical operational device is much more apparent for those countries existing on the peripheries of the world economy than for the fortunate few that coalesce around its core. South Africa, as a classic semi-peripheral state which relates to the northern core as an exporter of primary products and importer of high-grade technology, machinery and invest-ment, is therefore highly vulnerable to, and directly dependent on, the vagaries of global economic relations.

For this reason alone, South Africa's foreign policy options into the millennium will impact in a crucial way on how successfully the incoming government can consolidate the post-apartheid revolution and achieve its overall macroeconomic strategy, the primary purpose of which must be to foster a fast-growing economy in order to provide jobs, welfare, security and sustainable development for all its citizens.

## The ANC and international relations

Barring an electoral miracle, the ANC will remain the overwhelming political force in South Africa well into the twenty-first century. So dominant is it that despite the pluralist political framework provided by a liberal non-racial constitution, many even now fear that South Africa is, *de facto*, a single-party state. To understand the general outline of the country's foreign policy therefore, we need to consider the evolution of the ANC's international thinking from its founding in 1912 to the capture of power in 1994. Against this broad backdrop, it should then be possible to identify the current state of play and the kinds of foreign policy choices available to Thabo Mbeki's incoming administration.

Whereas the foreign policy orientation of the old South Africa from 1948 to 1994 was dramatically simple – it was a single-issue affair revolving around strategies to ensure the survival of the white regime – foreign policy in the new South Africa is a very complex matter. This is true not just of overall aims and objectives but also of the formulation and implementation of policy itself.

The ANC alliance is an extremely complicated ideological package. At least three distinct developmental phases impacted on policy-making during the organi-zation's first term of office: liberal internationalist (1912–60), socialist (1960–93) and pragmatist (from 1993). While these paradigm shifts are chronological, with one phase succeeding another, usually in response to external stimuli – exile in the

1960s, the collapse of the Cold War in the early 1990s – in policy terms they over-lap. It is therefore possible to discern elements of all three traditions of thought in the formulation and conduct of the GNU's foreign policy since 1994.[2]

Indeed, the alleged confusion in post-apartheid South Africa as to the nature of foreign policy and the kinds of roles the state should adopt in the region and in the wider world is in no small part attributable to the pull/push effects of this competing triad of theoretical perspectives and the lack of consensus within the ranks of the ruling party that has been generated by the consequent tensions. The result is that foreign policy is often argued out within a context of competing and often mutually exclusive perspectives – for example, pragmatic demands that ties with Europe and North America ought to be paramount, set against socialist and idealist demands that policy ought to be ethical, solidarist and Afro-centric.

One of the reasons, therefore, for the confusing policy signals coming from Pretoria since 1994 – especially concerning relations with its neighbours, with the European Union over access to the Lomé trade conventions, with the USA over solidarity with Cuba, Lybia, Syria, the Palestinians and Iran, and ambivalence over relations with Sudan, Algeria, Morocco and Indonesia – is that South Africa's post-Cold War and post-apartheid identity, and its conception of where its national interests lie, are still in the process of gestation. The ANC as the ruling party has not yet resolved the basic contradictions that have bedevilled its international thinking since it came to power. Thabo Mbeki's main foreign policy task during the first period of his presidency (which on present estimates might extend to a second term ending in 2009) will be to address this problem of policy drift or incoherence by forging a working consensus among the adherents of these competing perspectives. In particular he must assuage the fears of alliance partners, the SACP and COSATU, which continue to follow separate though overlapping agendas and as such offer distinctive inputs into policy-making.

## Foreign policy confusion and profusion, 1994–9

Mbeki and his deputy Aziz Pahad have long been aware of this problem and in fact began the process of policy reappraisal and 'new thinking' during the transition period. They realized in the wake of the demise of the USSR that, despite the inter-national standing of Nelson Mandela, by 1992–3 the ANC's continued attatchment to revolutionary socialist ideas about domestic and international affairs was widely perceived, both inside and outside South Africa, to be atavistic and anachronistic.

---

[2] The best general account of the ANC's international thinking is S. Thomas, *The Diplomacy of Liberation: The Foreign Relations of the ANC Since 1960* (London: Tauris, 1996). For a further exposition of the various theoretical phases see G. Evans, 'South Africa in Remission: the Foreign Policy of an Altered State', *Journal of Modern African Studies*, Summer 1996.

During this critical period, unlike the public relations-conscious de Klerk govern-ment, the ANC appeared totally out of step with a changing international order in which Western values of liberal democracy allied to the free market, a multiparty system and the notion of peaceful change within a culture of political toleration had now become universally accepted norms. During 1993–4, therefore, in a series of in-house party discussion documents, Mbeki began to distance the organization from its commitment to socialist ideas and moved to articulate policy programmes which converged with the post-Cold War neo-liberal international system. This involved recognition, at least in theory, of unipolarity, globalization, the importance of geo-economics, the general marginalization of Africa and its decidedly peripheral status in the global economy.

This pragmatic third phase has ensured that the ANC in office has not embarked on the kind of radical initiatives associated with policy pledges made in exile (such as nationalization of state assets and affirmative action programmes for the region). Although remnants of the old thinking did survive – solidarity with 'rogue states', for example – the general trend among Pretoria's new diplomatic community following Mbeki's bold lead has been to view foreign policy as an interest-based, pragmatic activity rather than as an exercise in the projection of ethical values or ideological principles.

Despite this shift, during President Mandela's administration foreign policy remained essentially contested territory within the diverse ranks of the ANC alliance. While Mandela himself understandably opted for an 'ethical' foreign policy, the main division during 1994–9 was between second-phase populists and ideologues and third-phase pragmatists and neo-liberals. This ongoing debate has served to frustrate the development of a coherent world-view and the accusations of vacilla-tion, ineffectualness and 'ad hocery' in foreign policy can largely be explained in terms of this historical tension.

Between 1994 and 1999, post-revolutionary fervour associated with liberation politics resulted in normative and theoretical confusion about proper foreign policy goals and objectives. Over and above this lack of agreement about fundamentals, South Africa also suffered from a profusion of decision-making centres and actors, each equipped with separate agendas and operating in competition with the others.

At the first-tier level of government, the presidential and vice-presidential offices, senior party officials, the Department of Foreign Affairs, the Defence, Safety and Security, Interior, Finance and Trade Ministries, the diplomatic corps and the Portfolio Committee on Foreign Affairs in the National Assembly all competed vigorously for the privilege of conducting the new South Africa's foreign relations. In the second tier of government, provincial elites often adopted unilateral, highly localized initiatives, especially in the crucial issue areas of trade and commerce (such as Mpumalanga's dealings with Mozambique and Gauteng's overtures to

Cuba). The inevitable foreign policy muddle emerging from this disaggregated process resulted in uncertainty both at home and abroad about the trajectory of South Africa's re-entry into world politics and its likely future direction. In fact, so serious was this problem that some critics observed that the new South Africa had no foreign policy at all – and even that was mismanaged. Notwithstanding these highly politicized attacks on the GNU, it remains true that the plethora of organizations, agencies, interest groups and personalities involved in foreign policy projection added to the confusion surrounding Pretoria's international relations.

The end of Nelson Mandela's presidency should open up more diplomatic space at both institutional and ideational levels for the incoming administration. South Africa will no doubt remain a symbol of the Third World struggle for liberation, human rights and distributive global economic justice. After all, Thabo Mbeki himself has a long and honourable place in the struggle against apartheid. Significantly, he also has an astute grasp of the causes of the structural asymmetry of international economic relations. His wide experience, both academically and practically, indicates that he is all too aware that the global economic game is rigged. However, unlike his distinguished predecessor, he does not carry the restrictive burden of being one of the heroes of the twentieth century. As a man, not a saint, his policy choices and margins should therefore be much more amenable to rational cost–benefit assessments unencumbered by fixed normative principles or by grand populist expectations.

## The future: Thabo Mbeki and the African Renaissance

What, then, are the prospects for the new administration? Clearly, Mbeki will be anxious from the outset to consolidate his grip on all aspects of policy-making. He is aware of the pressing need to resolve the continuing problems of conflicting perspectives and the lack of effective institutional arrangements for securing agreement on policy positions. With this in mind, he is likely to continue, and indeed to strengthen, the historical South African tradition of strong executive leadership in foreign affairs – a tradition which stretches back at least to the days of Jan Christian Smuts.[3]

In practical policy terms, he is likely to display a greater sensibility to Western free-market susceptibilities and interests than his predecessor. His support for GEAR, which signals acceptance of the neo-liberal orthodoxy in economic affairs, shows that he is not afraid of making difficult decisions and, if necessary, facing off elements within the SACP and COSATU who remain wedded to second-phase

---

[3] See D. Geldenhuys, 'The Heads of Government and South Africa's Foreign Relations', in R. Shrire (ed.), *From Malan to de Klerk: Leadership in the Apartheid State* (London: Hurst and Co., 1994).

radicalism. As a shrewd politician and modernizer, he shares with his British Labour counterpart Tony Blair a desire to construct a 'Third Way' between deeply entrenched and polarized positions. He recognizes that achieving fiscal stability and the sustainability of welfare spending involves greater market liberalization, and closer integration with the global economy.

While Mbeki acknowledges the saliency of the radical view that South Africa is part of the global South in world politics and is therefore a 'revisionist' state committed to amending the institutional, legal and economic regimes which were created by the North and which serve to sustain its global dominance, he is likely to pursue these goals through a combination of quiet diplomacy and assertive multilateralism. This will militate against adventurous or romantic postures of confrontation and defiance. As Nelson Mandela's ethical foreign policy showed all too clearly, heroic initiatives can often lead to outcomes where, paradoxically, the best becomes the enemy of the good.

Constrained by the restrictive domestic framework imposed by domestic priorities, Mbeki is aware of the costs incurred by pursuing politics not firmly grounded in the economic determinants of development, growth and prosperity. Consequently, anything which increases South Africa's risk rating and diminishes the prospect of international inward investment will be approached with caution.

However, it would be a mistake to think that Mbeki will jettison his radical past altogether. Thirty years spent as a leading member of the SACP, twenty-eight of them in exile, must have left its mark on this most enigmatic of politicians. Even accepting the veracity of his road-to-Damascus conversion to liberal orthodoxy in the early 1990s, for purely party political reasons he will need to appease the 'troublesome priests' in the alliance who continue to keep faith with doctrinal commitments entered into during the long diaspora. This means that he must give substance to the idea of the 'African Renaissance' which he has done so much to propagate since his nomination as Mandela's heir-apparent in 1997. Critics may argue that the African Renaissance, like Blair's concept of 'cool Britannia', is little more than a Clintonesque bumper-sticker with warm, evocative overtones but minimal intellectual or operational content. Moreover, recent developments might suggest that even at its launch this notion of political renewal, regeneration and third-wave democracy lies dead, at least in the fetid waters north of the Limpopo river. The more cynical might add that Thabo Mbeki's repeated protestations of his 'African-ness' have much the same significance and veracity as the routine declarations of 'Irishness' by the ubiquitous Boston-ward politician in the USA. But as well as being unduly sceptical and mischievous, these observations are highly misleading.

The idea of an African Renaissance may well be ambiguous and somewhat inscrutable, but it does resonate with a wide constituency in South and southern Africa.[4] Additionally, his commitment to 'African ways of dealing with African problems' should not be underestimated. At the very least, these two themes reinforce Mbeki's determination to counter the pervasive Afro-pessimism that the end of the Cold War brought in its wake. Indeed, this visionary historical metaphor could well come to symbolize the beginning of the ANC's fourth developmental phase in foreign policy thinking. For during the next five years we are likely to witness a more confident attempt by Pretoria to maximize its diplomatic and economic profile in Africa and to seek support from its neighbours and the OAU for permanent representation on the UN Security Council.

Renaissance diplomacy,[5] properly understood, must involve less emphasis on attention-grabbing universalism, and more on the more prosaic constraints imposed by local conditions: in this case the African diplomatic tradition of respect for its colonially crafted boundaries and the juridicial rights associated with territoriality and state sovereignty. This pragmatic, self-reliant view does not, of course, rule out a reappraisal of the sacrosanct OAU doctrine of non-intervention. Should a revision of this kind be prudent (and all indications are that this cannot be far away), the record suggests that Mbeki would sensibly run for the long grass of multilateralism and continentalism. While this might signal a greater willingness to embrace the repertoire of *realpolitik* than Mandela would be comfortable with, the approach does have the undoubted advantage of being sensitive to African developmental needs and of distancing South Africa from Western agendas and the interests of the major industrialized democracies.

For the past five years, South Africa has been hesitant to articulate a clear policy position on Africa. Its extreme sensitivity to charges of hegemonic ambitions means it has preferred to avoid individual responsibility for regional development. Instead, it has sought to wrap itself around the less risky option of bi- and mutilateralism. Recently, however, especially within its own national security and economic zones, there are signs that Mbeki is prepared to adopt a more proactive leadership role, although this will not be at the cost of developing the home base. The GEAR programme will continue to drive policy. Mbeki is aware that five years down the road from apartheid the inescapable priority for South Africa is domestic reconstruction and economic growth allied to internal social and political stability. Foreign policy – debts to neighbours incurred while in exile notwithstanding – will not be allowed to compromise this goal. Accordingly South Africa's international profile over the next five years must generate tangible material pay-offs.

It is not fanciful, therefore, to interpret the African Renaissance idea as representing Thabo Mbeki's grand design to re-invent South Africa as a global trading state with strong regional and continental interests – a trading state, moreover,

[4] See P. Vale and S. Maseko, 'South Africa and the African Renaissance', *International Affairs*, Vol. 74, No. 2, April 1998, pp. 271–89.
[5] See G. Mattingly, *Renaissance Diplomacy* (London: Cape, 1955).

which exists fortuitously at the intersection of four overlapping foreign policy circles: sub-Saharan Africa, continental Africa, the Western world and the Indian Ocean/ Pacific Rim. South Africa is an indispensable link between these disparate economic and ideological entities, and its diplomatic mission will be to maintain, as far as is practicable, an active presence in all four realms while reserving the right to play one off against another and prioritize as circumstances may require.

The objective would appear to be to work within the constraints imposed by the international economy while pursuing what opportunities for growth this may throw up. This doctrine, which could be termed *four-circle internationalism* or *omni-balancing*, implies a quest to obtain maximum economic concessions from as many regional blocs as possible while simultaneously concentrating on the areas within which it has the competitive edge – the southern African sub-region where it maintains a 5:1 trade surplus based on the export of manufactured goods. The logic of this position dictates that a winning strategy would be to pursue policies designed to wrest concessions from the global core and at the same time to enlarge its share of the African market. This should represent a foreign policy that it is coherent, affordable, supportable and in the best interests of the country as a whole. South Africa's recent carefully calibrated intercession in the Lockerbie affair is clearly a pointer to this new sense of diplomatic maturity and confidence. It also reinforces South Africa's self-image as a responsible and reliable leading player in the politics of the global South.

Strategically, the strength of the Renaissance idea is that it enables Pretoria to reconcile the twin post-Cold War imperatives of globalization and localization. Tactically, this Third Way, with its emphasis on radicalism *and* moderation, should satisfy the solidarist factions within the ANC alliance and the more pragmatic desires of South Africa's increasingly strident new 'merchants of Venice'. In sum, the foreign policy orientation of Thabo Mbeki's incoming administration will involve a judicious mix of Machiavellian *virtù* and Enlightenment emancipatory ideas. As such, the leitmotif of his diplomacy will be interest defined in terms of economic development, expressed within the custodial framework provided by the primacy of domestic politics and a high-profile commitment to the Republic's African heritage and destiny.

# B: SOUTH AFRICA'S RELATIONS WITH THE WEST

## *James Barber*

Within the international community Western powers and values are currently in the ascendant. This is particularly striking in global economic relations. South Africa's major economic partners are Western – the United States, Japan and the European Union (notably Germany and Britain; see Tables 1 and 2). The major global institutions which set the financial and trading agendas – the World Bank, the IMF, the G7 and the World Trade Organization – reflect Western values and assumptions. For the foreseeable future South Africa, which in global terms has a small economy, has little choice but to accept the situation, irrespective of who forms its government. Reflecting this global situation, the Republic is developing a mixed economy, in which private companies and the government both have prominent roles. This is not what many ANC members envisaged during the long years of the liberation struggle, when socialist influences became increasingly prominent. That came to an end with the collapse of the East European bloc and the Soviet Union. Although an internal debate continues within the ANC, the leadership accepts that to gain international trade, investment and aid it must tread the Western economic path.

**Table 1:  South Africa's top trading partners, 1996/7 (million rand)**

|  | 1996 | | | 1997 | | |
|---|---|---|---|---|---|---|
|  | Total trade | SA imports | SA exports | Total trade | SA imports | SA exports |
| UK | 28,421 | 14,972 | 13,449 | 31,773 | 14,642 | 17,131 |
| US | 25,625 | 15,1379 | 9,746 | 27,341 | 16,151 | 11,190 |
| Germany | 26,089 | 20,436 | 5,653 | 24,212 | 17,614 | 6,598 |
| Japan | 22,331 | 13,026 | 9,305 | 19,344 | 9,652 | 9,692 |

*Source:* South African Institute of International Affairs, *Yearbook 1998/9* (Johannesburg, 1998), p. 387.

**Table 2: Foreign investment in South Africa at end 1997 (billion rand)**

|  | Total investment (direct & indirect) | Direct investment | Indirect investment |
|---|---|---|---|
| Total | 305.865 | 89.295 | 216.570 |
| UK | 103.747 | 37.345 | 66.402 |
| US | 61.535 | 12.953 | 48.582 |
| Germany | 31.215 | 12.278 | 18.937 |

*Source*: South African Reserve Bank data.

The Western impact can also be seen in political and cultural developments. South Africa's multi-party democracy, the supremacy of the constitution, regular free elections and a strong civil society also reflect Western institutions and values. Finally, the ubiquitous Western culture is found in education, films, television, books, music and clothes. However, that is not to imply either that the influence is all one-way, or that the new South Africa is a client state of the West. It is not. It has its own distinctive qualities and political views. That has been demonstrated by President Mandela's refusal to distance himself from Cuba and Libya; Pretoria's criticism of the US and British policy on Iraq; the refusal to kow-tow to Western ideas on African security; and the challenge to some of the implications of Western-dominated economic globalization. In January 1999, President Mandela told the World Economic Forum, at Davos, Switzerland, that globalization was not a panacea for all economic ills, and while it might be profitable for some market players, it could be destructive for developing countries. If the needs of the developing world were not taken into account, he said, it would lead to global instability and even conflict.[1]

The new South Africa's distinctive international role is further illustrated in insti-tutional terms, as it emerges as a Third World leader. It currently chairs the Non-Aligned Movement; it is gaining increasing prominence in general African affairs; and it has aspirations for a permanent seat on a reconstructed UN Security Council. Seen from the West, South Africa is one of the few post-Cold War success stories. The West therefore listens to and is eager to support Pretoria both to gain reflected glory from the South African 'miracle', and to build on the success by improving the situation across Africa. Further Pretoria can act as a valuable link for the West as it seeks to resolve long-standing problems with 'difficult' non-Western states. Two examples of this are the 'go-between' role that South Africa has played in resolving the Lockerbie dispute with Libya, and the East Timor conflict with Indonesia.

## The United States and South Africa

Relations with the United States illustrate the mixed pattern of contacts. For a variety of reasons Washington is eager to promote a successful, prosperous South Africa – to help stabilize the continent, to act as an African peacekeeper and dynamo for development, to provide a market for American goods, to symbolize the success of democratic institutions, and to satisfy its Afro-American constituency at home. For these ends, and to signal the importance it places on Pretoria, the United States has established a Binational Commission (so far chaired by Al Gore and Thabo Mbeki) to promote cooperation in trade, investment, energy, agriculture, education and technology. Yet an element of tension exists alongside the cooper-

---

[1] South African government press release of speech on 29 January 1999.

ation. Washington's aid programme is its largest in Africa, but the South Africans believe it should be much larger (President Mandela once described it as 'peanuts'). Although it gives aid Washington's emphasis is on private enterprise. US officials preach that bringing and encouraging this as well as trade are the best contribution Americans can make. This is a less attractive picture for Pretoria. The cards seem stacked in favour of the United States, with which South Africa runs a substantial trade deficit ($800 million in 1998, while the aid programme is $80 million), and which controls the capital for investment.

The mixture of cooperation and tension is also present in political and diplomatic relations. Bilateral relations between the two governments are excellent, but there are differences over relations with other states, including Libya and Cuba, and US policy in the Middle East. This mixture is likely to continue, but Mandela's retirement could have the contradictory impact of reducing the differences that were highlighted by Mandela's status while also giving them a sharper edge than had been apparent from the forgiving attitude towards Mandela.

There are similar characteristics in South Africa's relations with other major Western states, but in each case there are distinctive qualities – none more so than in relations with the United Kingdom.

## Britain and South Africa

When Tony Blair visited South Africa in January 1999, the British spin was on 'the new' and 'the future'. In an article for the local press Maeve Fort, the British High Commissioner, wrote that Britain 'is no longer a country of sedate afternoon teas and bowler hats', but rather of advanced technology and modern design companies. The new British government, she stated, looked to the future rather than the past.[2] It was in that light that one of Blair's objectives was to cement his relations with Thabo Mbeki, 'the President in waiting' . On his arrival Blair declared: 'Because of his [Mbeki's] leadership qualities I have great confidence in the future here.' He spoke of South Africa as a leading economy, as a peace-maker and peacekeeper, and as a force for good in the continent. A diverse agenda was announced for the formal meetings, including British investment and aid to South Africa, developments across the continent, the Lockerbie air disaster, and the 2006 Football World Cup.

On the whole Blair achieved his aims: his personal meetings with Mbeki went well; he announced an increase of 40 per cent in British aid over the next three years (R900 million in all); he spoke hopefully of British investments worth 4 billion linked to a major arms order for British aircraft; and the South Africans agreed to use their good offices with Libya over the Lockerbie affair.

[2] *Star and SA Times*, 6 January 1999.

Yet not all went as planned. Blair was met on arrival by two demonstrations, neither of which fitted his agenda. The larger one – which was broken up by police using a water cannon and plastic bullets – was by Muslims protesting at US/British policy towards Iraq and in particular the recent bombing raids. The protest not only underlined the readiness of militant Muslim groups to act anywhere, it also exposed a policy difference between London and Pretoria, for Pretoria opposed the bombing. The other demonstration was by Afrikaners, protesting at the concentration camps used by the British in the Boer War, almost 100 years before. That was a reminder that, despite Blair's stress on the future, Anglo-South African relations are and will continue to be influenced by the past. The two countries are linked by their shared history. Douglas Hurd, when Foreign Secretary, described the relationship as 'an historic and persistent interest' for Britain.[3] However, ever since Britain occupied the Cape during the Napoleonic wars (to protect the sea route to the East), it has been a stressful as well as a persistent interest. The stress has continued into the recent past. Contrasting images spring to mind – the 'arms to South Africa' controversy of the Wilson and Heath governments; sports boycotts; agents of apartheid bombing of the ANC's London headquarters; Margaret Thatcher swinging her handbag in opposition to economic sanctions; and anti-apartheid demonstrations in Trafalgar Square. As a result South Africa has penetrated the British consciousness. The experience is mutual, for Britain has featured and continues to feature large in South Africa. With Mandela's retirement some of the glamour will disappear and the two sides may become less tolerant of each other's idiosyncrasies, but the consciousness will remain. The interplay with the past can be illustrated in terms of personal contacts, cultural and sporting links, economic activity and government-to-government relations.

Personal links between South Africa and Britain are myriad – family ties, two-way immigration, business contacts, students and academic exchanges, friendships, visitors and tourists – with the English language providing an important common bond. Such contacts are important for the future, in terms of the South Africa tourist industry, and for British citizens living in South Africa.

With justification Pretoria has great hopes that its tourist industry will play a significant part in the country's economic development. The tourist potential is enormous, and since 1990 Westerners, with the British in the lead, have responded in growing numbers. In addition to the routine tourist industry, South Africa is promoting itself vigorously as a centre for international events, especially in sport. Already it has staged the world rugby cup, made an unsuccessful Olympic bid, and is now hoping to land the world football cup. There are physical limitations to these high ambitions, but the greatest problem is South Africa's growing notoriety as a

[3] House of Commons Foreign Affairs Committee, *UK Policy Towards South Africa*, February 1991, Vol. 2, p. 8.

place of murder, physical violence and theft. The Republic now has contrasting images in Britain as the land of a political miracle (with President Mandela a living legend) and a land of crime. If the crime image persists it will undermine hopes for the expansion of the tourist industry and the staging of international events.

Crime may also be a factor in the future of British citizens living in the Republic. If British ministers have nightmares about South Africa they will be related to a rapid flight of people to the UK. The number of British passport holders living in South Africa is estimated to be about 300,000; including dependants there could be up to 700,000 people with the right of settlement in Britain. Nobody suggests that anything like that number would arrive at any one time, but the concern exists. A major economic downturn in South Africa, difficulty in finding jobs because of positive discrimination in favour of blacks, and increasing disorder and crime could all provoke an extensive exodus, which would create problems for both societies. South Africa would lose skilled workers, and Britain would gain people who might find difficulty in fitting into a new society. If for no other reason, it is in Britain's interests to promote a peaceful and prosperous South Africa.

## Economic relations and the European Union

In overall terms – trade, investment, aid, companies operating in one another's territory, and number of employees – Britain is South Africa's major economic partner. For example, while in 1998 US companies operating in South Africa directly employed about 71,000 people, British companies employed 128,000. The common interests which flow from this will be important in the future as in the past. South African exporters, not least in the agricultural sector, will continue to look to the UK as a major market; while British companies will look for investment opportunities and markets for a range of manufactured goods. However, it is a constantly shifting scene, as illustrated by the behaviour of individual companies and the institutional framework in which economic contact takes place.

Companies trade and invest in search of profit, not on sentiment, in a world in which there is strong competition for Western trade and investment. These are hard lessons for the new South Africa. Thus issues as wide-ranging as the tax regime, the repatriation of profits, corruption, inflation and security for company plant employees come into play. So far the Republic has just about held its own in this competitive world, but it has failed to gain the scale of investment leading to an economic lift-off which would make substantial inroads into its unemployment problem. It will probably continue to struggle in future.

In terms of its institutional framework much Anglo-South African trade is now shaped by British membership of the EU. Since 1994 South Africa and the EU have conducted prolonged and tortuous negotiations in search of a trade agreement.

Britain has generally supported South Africa's position, because of their long-standing relationship and because, given their complementary economies, it is in its interests to do so. Some other EU states have been less sympathetic. That is partly because of South Africa's dual economy (with its First and Third World elements), and partly because South Africa is seen as a rival by EU states with similar agricultural products – France, Spain, Portugal, Italy and Greece. The result was a series of disputes – including over South Africa's qualifications for Lomé trade terms; the import into the EU of steel and a range of agricultural products; relations with other southern African states; and the use of the names 'port' and 'sherry'. Until the last moment it appeared that the negotiations might collapse. In February 1999 Tony Blair warned that if they did fail the EU's relations not only with South Africa but with the whole African continent would be adversely affected. However, a free trade agreement has now been hammered out. Assuming no further pitfalls lie ahead, the agreement should, over the next ten years, free or greatly open up trade and investment opportunities. Yet some barriers remain. The most significant is the EU's Common Agricultural Policy, which places a protective shield around European farm products. In his speech to the World Economic Forum, President Mandela picked this out for special mention as unfair competition against developing countries. He might have added that the negotiations have taught the new government in Pretoria that for all the Western public enthusiasm for South Africa's political 'miracle' and for President Mandela personally, when it comes to international bargaining self-interest usually prevails.

Anglo-South African relations at government level are close and friendly. There is a coincidence of interests on many issues. Both governments are eager to encourage economic contacts, both are enthusiastic Commonwealth members, there are good personal relations between leaders on both sides, and both share broader interests in Africa. Britain recognizes South Africa as a continental giant, especially in southern Africa. Most of the states in the region are former British possessions and now Commonwealth members. Therefore, both London and Pretoria share the ambition to see a prosperous and settled region. To that end Britain will continue to gear its aid programme towards achieving both economic development and political security.

On the security front Britain has provided military training for several southern African states. In South Africa's case this has been directed at helping to integrate the defence forces from the old apartheid regime and the liberation movements, and to train South African forces for peacekeeping operations elsewhere on the continent. Such collaboration characterizes existing government-to-government relations. Although, as noted above, there are differences between Pretoria and London, and once Mandela goes South Africa is unlikely to gain as much attention in Britain, relations between the two governments are so good that a senior British official confessed: 'We often have to rack our brains to find issues on which we disagree.'

## C: SOUTH AFRICA'S ROLE IN INTERNATIONAL PEACEKEEPING

### *James Mayall*

Since 1994, South Africa has been reluctant to commit forces to international peacekeeping operations, but has actively pursued political solutions to international crises by diplomatic means, particularly in Africa. The results have not been impressive, whether in Nigeria, where President Mandela's quiet diplomacy failed to save Ken Saro-Wiwa and the other Ngoni activists from 'judicial murder', or in former Zaire, where Laurent Kabila effectively ignored South African efforts to broker an agreement with the former President Mobutu. Critics of the ANC government, within South Africa, have blamed the ANC for failing to develop a coherent foreign policy, and even for squandering its greatest foreign policy asset, namely Mandela's personal moral stature. When it finally did use military force in August 1998 – to head off a military coup in Lesotho – the operation was ill-prepared, heavy-handed and poorly executed, leading one commentator to quip that 'South Africa moved from democracy to ad-hocracy, and appeared to be making its foreign policy up as it went along'.

Should we expect a government led by President Thabo Mbeki to do better? The argument of this section is that while there may be demands for a more proactive South African peacekeeping policy, the constraints under which the next South African government will operate will be much the same as those faced by its predecessor. Indeed, to the extent that the ANC leadership ponder the lessons of the 'botched' intervention in Lesotho, they may well conclude that, for the time being, they should be even more cautious about deploying South African forces beyond the country's borders. On the other hand, the argument that Mandela's government lacked a coherent foreign policy is not particularly compelling. Most countries make up their foreign policy as they go along, mainly because though their interests may remain constant, the circumstances to which they must react are not. South Africa's reluctance to get involved in peacekeeping operations has general and specific causes which we will consider shortly. But it does not follow that, because these still apply, a Mbeki government will necessarily be able to resist intervention in all circumstances.

## Peacekeeping in the 1990s

At the time of the 1994 elections, there was considerable enthusiasm for the idea that South Africa should play a major role in international peace-support operations. In part this reflected a triumphalist view within the ANC, an understandable feeling that South Africa's experience of successfully negotiating its own democratic transition could be used as a model for peace-building in other deeply divided, conflict-prone African societies. It also reflected external pressure on South Africa, following the 'failure' of United Nations peacekeeping in Somalia and Rwanda. Initial enthusiasm faded as the government assessed both risks and costs, and realized that the South African National Defence Force (SANDF) lacked the necessary training and experience. The 1996 Defence White Paper set out the conditions that would have to be met before South Africa would participate in peace support operations. These conditions are unlikely to be relaxed after the elections. They are:

1. There should be parliamentary approval and public support for such involvement. This will require an appreciation of the associated costs and risks, including financial costs and risks to the lives of military personnel.
2. The operation should have a clear mandate, mission and objectives.
3. There should be realistic criteria for terminating the operation.
4. The operation should be authorized by the UN Security Council.
5. Operations in Southern Africa should be sanctioned by the Southern African Development Community[1] and undertaken with other SADC states, rather than be conducted on a unilateral basis. Similarly, operations in Africa should be sanctioned by the OAU.

To maintain its ethical foreign policy, South Africa had taken cover behind the United Nations. By 1996 the Security Council was in retreat from the forward position it had adopted with regard to peacekeeping in the early 1990s. The South African conditions for participation bear a strong family resemblance to those being developed at the time by the major troop-providing powers. It is important to recognize, therefore, that there are general reasons for South Africa's caution. When, in 1994, the UN reduced the size of its force in Rwanda and deliberately refrained from referring to the Tutsi massacres as a genocide, it faced a bleak reality: none of the nineteen countries that had previously offered forces for a peacekeeping operation, on the assumption that the Arusha Peace Accords would be implemented, were prepared to intervene in a ferocious civil conflict where there was no peace to keep. Peacekeeping is expensive and governments are increasingly wary of taking on new commitments. But the real constraint is not the money but the mandate – no one has yet conceived a way of intervening in a civil conflict and remaining impartial at the same time.

[1] The SADC comprises (as of January 1999): Angola, Botswana, Democratic Republic of Congo, Lesotho, Malawi, Mauritius, Mozambique, Namibia, Seychelles, South Africa, Swaziland, Tanzania, Zambia, and Zimbabwe.

Once the major Western powers recognized that they could face an explosion of demands to establish peacekeeping operations around the world they quickly developed a preference for regionalization, a possibility that is allowed for under Chapter VIII of the UN Charter. The idea that there should be African solutions to African problems has been the policy of the Organization of African Unity from the beginning, but whatever its other merits, regionalization does not solve the mandate problem. There is no reason to believe that regional powers will be any more impartial in their own neighbourhood than outsiders. Indeed, the record of intervention both by ECOWAS in Liberia and by some SADC countries in the Congo suggests the opposite. South Africa is thus in good company in preferring prudence to adventurism in relation to African conflicts where its own interests are not directly engaged.

## Domestic constraints

South African reluctance to soldier abroad also has two powerful domestic sources. The first is an unwillingness to divert scarce resources from the formidable array of development and reconstruction projects within the country. Indeed, the defence budget has been slashed by around 25 per cent to direct resources in the opposite direction. The pressures to give priority to domestic reform are likely to be even greater on a Mbeki government than they were under Mandela, if only because as the apartheid era recedes, majority rule will no longer be sufficient to assuage popular discontent. Already in the summer of 1998, a series of ugly incidents involving the victimization of foreign workers provided evidence that the very high levels of unemployment could trigger xenophobia. Even if the problems arise solely from social and economic problems within South Africa, insofar as they involve foreign workers they may exacerbate regional tensions and rivalries. There will be a temptation for the country to retreat into isolation.

The second domestic constraint is concern over the state of the armed forces. Unlike some of its neighbours, for example Botswana, South Africa has had no opportunity to acquire the skills associated with international peacekeeping. Under apartheid the South African Defence Force (SADF) was responsible for defending the state against the anticipated onslaught from outside, and, more recently, for destabilizing the region by periodic intrusions into neighbouring countries. On the other side UmKontho weSiswe (MK), the ANC's armed wing, was trained to engage in low-intensity guerrilla warfare, although, in exile, it had little opportunity. Since 1994, the renamed South African National Defence Force has been reduced in size from the original SADF, and is currently being remodelled, with British assistance, through the integration of elements from both the SADF and the MK.

South Africa remains more formidably armed than most African states – it accounts for around 80 per cent of military expenditure in southern Africa. But it is not yet equipped or trained to undertake major peacekeeping responsibilities, outside its immediate neighbourhood. Even there, the evidence of the Lesotho operation suggests that much remains to be done to transform SANDF into an effective instrument for conflict resolution. By intervening, South Africa may have demonstrated its zero-tolerance of military coups in neighbouring countries, but the manner in which it shored up the elected government will not have boosted confidence elsewhere in the region where memories of earlier South African interventions persist.

Prior to the Lesotho débâcle, the South African government had aimed to keep its military power in reserve, and to concentrate on preventive diplomacy and peace-making. At least within the immediate region this approach was reasonably successful, reversing an earlier coup in Lesotho in 1994 and forcing RENAMO to participate in the Mozambique elections in 1996. Both at the multilateral level – it hosted the Non-Aligned Movement in 1998 and will host the Commonwealth summit in 1999 – and bilaterally, South Africa has committed itself to the democratization of international relations. The question that arises after the Lesotho intervention is whether its credibility on this score has been seriously damaged. It is too early to answer this question with any confidence. However, if a political solution is not forthcoming in the Democratic Republic of the Congo, or Sierra Leone, before South Africa takes the chair at the Commonwealth summit, the government will find itself under renewed pressure to provide effective leadership in dealing with African crises. Whether this can be done without military involvement is also unclear.

## Future prospects

The argument for more active involvement in peacekeeping exposes a dilemma which is bound to face any South African government for the foreseeable future. Which way should the country face? Should it give priority to Africa, to which it undeniably belongs, but which at present can contribute little to the solution of its economic and social problems? Or should it concentrate on the industrial West, whose capital it wishes to tap and whose market it cultivates? Vice-President Mbeki's high-profile campaign for an African Renaissance is a deliberate attempt to resolve this dilemma (see section by Graham Evans). On the one hand it espouses democratic political values, but on the other it sees democratization as the only way in which African societies can resolve their own problems and escape from neo-colonial dependence on the West.

So long as South Africa's contribution to crisis management can be essentially diplomatic, the government can handle the dilemma. The danger is that if South Africa becomes militarily entangled in African crises, it is likely to be seen as the proxy of the West, the United States in particular. This was presumably why

President Mandela refused to associate himself with the African Crisis Response Initiative (ACRI), the programme under which the United States is providing peacekeeping training and equipment to a number of African countries. The ANC remains suspicious of Western motives. A recent policy paper conceded that France and the United States were committed to resolving the problems of the Great Lakes region, but complained that 'they were also trying to resolve these problems in a way that strengthens their influence in that region, thus almost undermining the relatively peaceful transition in the former Zaire'.[2] A new government is unlikely to feel differently, particularly as American and British policy in Iraq has made it even more difficult to maintain a balancing act. But, given the renewed crisis in the Congo, it may find it harder to resist Western pressure for fuller participation. One indication that South Africans accept that they will eventually have to respond more positively to such pressure is the inclusion of a Security Committee in the Binational Commission which meets at cabinet level to promote US support for the democratic transition. Until 1997 they had refused all American requests for such a committee, but since its establishment there has also been a noticeable softening in government statements about the initiative.

## The impact of the Congo crisis

The continuing crisis in the Democratic Republic of the Congo is likely to present the Mbeki government with its severest test in the area of conflict management. It has even been suggested that the costly intervention in Lesotho was in reaction to goading by Mugabe's government in Zimbabwe and domestic critics about the government's refusal to go to the aid of the besieged President Kabila. South Africa's defence was that the two cases were not comparable: in Lesotho, the intervention, however inept, was to uphold a democratically elected government; in Congo, Kabila, whose path to office had been eased by South Africa eighteen months earlier, showed no signs of embarking on the democratic transitions he had promised.

Nonetheless, what the Congo crisis has undoubtedly achieved is a major fracture within SADC, the one regional organization in Africa which had previously seemed capable of constructing a viable framework for security and development. South Africa and Botswana – the two countries whose troops remain in Lesotho – have refused to intervene in the Congo, while Zimbabwe, Angola and Namibia have accepted Kabila's claim that he is the victim of aggression from Uganda and Rwanda.

The issues at stake are beyond the scope of this analysis. Suffice it to say that they have very little to do with peacekeeping or peace enforcement as traditionally

---

[2] 'Developing a Strategic Perspective on South African Foreign Policy', 27 December 1998 (http://www.anc.org.za/ancdocs/discussion/foreign.html).

understood. Whether or not the interventions are sanctioned by SADC is disputed by President Mandela, who is chairman of the organization, and President Mugabe, who heads its Organ on Politics, Defence and Security. Thabo Mbeki will inherit this unsatisfactory division of responsibility, which resulted from the rivalry between the two presidents. It is unlikely that he will easily be able to overcome it, partly because the whole region is now so heavily militarized, and partly because South Africa's membership of SADC has inevitably upset the internal balance of power within the organization. Indeed, one reason why Zaire was admitted was to balance South Africa and to move the regional centre of gravity northwards.

The intractability of the Congo conflict suggest that South Africa was wise to stand aloof. But it may yet destabilize the region in ways that will affect South African interests more directly and confront the new government with the need to take complex and difficult decisions. To date, South Africa's efforts to broker a political solution suggest that it has little appetite for them. In December 1998, Mbeki wrote to Paul Kagame, the Vice-President of Rwanda, proposing a cease-fire in which all troops would stay in their positions, and that subsequently 'the forces currently engaged in the military conflict ... [should] ... contribute units to a joint force of the belligerents to serve as a peacekeeping force'. The attempt to stimulate a debate which would address the real rather than the hypothetical security situation in the Congo, and reassure all the parties to the conflict, is praiseworthy; but a political solution is likely to need more concrete incentives than this. Within the region, the problem of South African hegemony will ultimately be difficult to avoid. All the more important, therefore, that, even if it is not loved, the country should be regarded with respect by its neighbours. Over the long run it would seem only prudent to prepare the SANDF to specialize in peace-support operations on lines developed by other middle-ranking powers such as Canada, Sweden and India.

# 7 CONCLUSIONS

## A: PROSPECTS FOR 2000 AND BEYOND

### Greg Mills

As South Africa moves away from the honeymoon period of the Mandela era to the strong prospect of a two-term (ten-year) Thabo Mbeki presidency, it will increasingly be judged not on its past history but rather on current achievements and future programmes. These will to a large extent also determine the success and direction of its foreign policy.

## Current strengths and future challenges

Here the successful management of the four so-called 'deficits' common to developing countries will shape South Africa's future: the fiscal deficit, down as a percentage of GDP from 10.1 per cent in 1993/4 to 4.2 per cent in 1997/8 and 3.9 per cent in 1998/9; the current account deficit, which doubled to 1.5 per cent over 1998, demanding high interest rates to attract inward capital flows and maintain monetary stability; the skills/efficiency/education deficit; and the social deficit. Critical to all of these is the ability of leadership to manage and implement policy – the type of pragmatic leadership which Africa has had in such short supply in the post-colonial period.

The government has failed to deliver in three key areas since 1994: economic growth, education and crime. For example, the real GDP growth rate was just 0.2 per cent in 1998, much lower than the originally anticipated level of 3 per cent. This is partly due to an unfavourable wider environment for emerging markets generally, but also reflects doubts about policy and leadership direction and reliability. Labour legislation, in particular, has been seen to be investor-unfriendly, while there are concerns, too, about Deputy President Mbeki's choice of personnel and his (excessive) focus on domestic politicking and safeguarding his position as heir-elect, at the expense of policy implementation. Since April 1994, Mbeki has expended much time in cementing his power-base, and in shaping his own policies and political philosophy – including, most famously, the foreign policy vision of an

'African Renaissance'(as discussed in the section by Graham Evans). But he has come under some criticism for his approach, being seen as inaccessible, complex and over-academic, even ponderous.

Although there has been progress in terms of service delivery (between 1994 and 1998, some 650,000 homes out of the government's promised total of one million had been constructed), concerns over delivery are compounded by an environment of high criminality and a failure to meet expectations. Polls show that South Africans remain equally divided on whether the country is going in the right direction, though the number of those who feel it is not has increased substantially since 1994.

An estimated 560,000 new jobs were, by 1998, needed each year to redress the high unemployment figure of three million and to provide for those entering the labour market. A failure to do so, combined with a high rate of AIDS infection, creates a cocktail for social dislocation and, possibly, populist politics. It is estimated that 10.4 per cent of South Africa's population is currently HIV-positive, a figure expected to rise to 12.5 per cent by 2006. As a result, the population growth rate will drop from its current rate, in the order of 2–2.5 per cent, to 0.7 per cent in 2006.

Yet South Africa continues to be blessed with a strong legal and financial system, a durable, democratic and effective government, tolerable levels of inflation and international trade exposure, low external debt and fiscal austerity. Key also is government's ongoing commitment to its conservative macro-economic reform strategy (GEAR). The downside is, however, reflected in the relatively high level of population expansion, low GDP growth, high unemployment, high interest rates and low external liquidity along with a volatile (and falling) currency value.

Investors remain sceptical of the government's relationship with its left-wing allies. This had led to contentious legislation such as the Labour Relations Act and the Employment Equity Act, which regulates the labour market and seeks, *inter alia*, to legislate affirmative action. The scepticism has been heightened by a combination of the fall-out from the Asian financial crisis for emerging markets generally and specific concerns over high rates of crime in South Africa. Low rates of productivity and high economic transaction costs also continued to deter foreign and local investors.

South Africa's past of racial oppression, violence and dehumanization, along with increasing inaccessibility to the material targets of crime and decreasing fear of punishment on the part of criminals, have combined to increase the violence of criminal acts in South Africa. Among Interpol reporting countries, South Africa is the worst country for rape; has the second highest rate of robbery with aggravating circumstances; and the third highest incidence of murder. The rate for murders of police officials is also among the highest in the world, with 120 in the first six months of 1998.

In spite of these difficulties, the political landscape is expected to remain stable. Political (rather than criminal) violence has diminished significantly since the early

1990s, down from 23,139 deaths between 1984 and 1996 to just 470 deaths in 1998. No obvious, serious challengers to either the ANC's or Thabo Mbeki's rule are on the horizon. Although the opposition political parties have focused their election campaigns on the need to prevent the ANC from obtaining a two-thirds parliamentary majority which would enable it to change the constitution unchallenged, in fact most of the opposition to ANC policies continues to come from its major allies within the government, notably the SACP and COSATU, rather than the other parliamentary parties. It is also true that there remain divisions within the ANC between the 'exiles' (who fought apartheid based mainly in South Africa's neighbouring states and in European capitals) and those who cut their teeth in South Africa's extra-parliamentary groups – the trade unions, the now-disbanded United Democratic Front (which essentially operated as an internal wing of the ANC from 1983 to 1990), and other elements of civil society.

## Foreign policy

South Africa's foreign relations have been a matter of intense public debate since the advent of its democracy in 1994. Nearly five years after the end of isolation, the portfolio is seen as one of the worst performing in government.

There have been many questions asked in the Republic about the country's foreign policy direction and progress, and the role of political leadership. South Africa's Minister of Foreign Affairs, Alfred Nzo, has consistently been ranked as one of the poorest performers in the cabinet. This may be one reason for the comparatively slow pace of departmental reform. Only in mid-1998 was the first, post-apartheid Director-General of the Department of Foreign Affairs (DFA) appointed in the person of Jackie Selebi. In the policy domain, the ruling ANC has somewhat clumsily attempted to juggle a number of ideological and practical priorities: the need to ensure economic growth and socio-political stability in South Africa through developing existing and new trade and investment relationships; the imperative to form a mutually beneficial relationship with Africa, especially its southern African neighbours; along with the wider imperative of consolidating relations with the developing, or non-aligned world.

In fairness, the foreign service has faced something of a tall order. First, at a bureaucratic level, the government has expanded its diplomatic missions from under 30 in 1990 to over 90 today. This, one official has noted, was a 'bewildering' exercise and 'a steep learning curve'. Second, given President Mandela's international profile and South Africa's comparatively giant continental status, South Africa has been expected to take the lead on international issues, even if sometimes only by default. Here policy has tended to follow the personality rather than vice versa. Third, the Republic has been somewhat reluctant to define its own national interests and stamp these on its relations with its partners in the developing world, many of which have sought to retain political leverage by highlighting their role in the anti-apartheid struggle. In its relations with the 14 member-states of the Southern African Development Community, this has led to a perception in government that South Africa 'was damned if it did, and damned if it didn't'. Pretoria has (unsurprisingly) often been expected to take the policy lead in the region, but in turn has been singled out for criticism over its 'hegemonic' behaviour.

It would, however, be uncharitable to suggest that South Africa has been altogether without its foreign policy successes. Pretoria's role in crafting an indefinite, conditional extension to the nuclear Non-Proliferation Treaty in New York in May 1995 has been complemented by positive actions elsewhere in the arms control and disarmament community – in terms of the role, for example, played by Selebi when South African Ambassador to the UN in Geneva in chairing the Oslo meeting that established the terms and conditions for a global landmine ban. The success of Pretoria's chairmanship, from 1995, of the UN Conference on Trade and Development (UNCTAD) is now echoed in the early stages of its new and less polemical leadership of the Non-Aligned Movement which it assumed at the Durban summit in August–September 1998.

Under Selebi's dynamic mantle, the DFA has taken a grip on the challenges posed by the post-Mandela world, and has undertaken the ambitious task of both transforming the foreign service and making South Africa's foreign policy 'predictable'. The making of foreign policy is, of course, no different to other areas of government activity. There is a need, first, to establish policy priorities, and, second, to devise a systematic way – a strategy – of achieving these goals. Critical in the latter regard are two factors: resources and the willingness to make hard political choices.

Reflecting Thabo Mbeki's concept of a South African foreign policy built on two pillars – one each in the developing and developed worlds – the DFA now argues for a higher profile and more assertive action by the foreign service in both wealth creation (through, *inter alia*, a coordinated approach to globalization, the enhancement of South Africa's image abroad, and the vigorous pursuit of trade and investment) and security (through the promotion of compliance with international law, and active engagement in conflict prevention, management and resolution).

The DFA has identified thirteen themes or policy areas, and the strategies within these are to be prioritized and defined by the input of both an embryonic DFA Policy Planning Unit and through the feedback of regional desks and missions. Underlying the creation of wealth and security is an appeal for South Africa to promote democratization and human rights. Put simply, this process attempts to link foreign policy with domestic needs and values, and to restructure the foreign service around defined goals.

But what about making the hard political choices in the face of a lack of human and financial resources? Although they faced a steep learning curve in 1994 in carrying out a threefold expansion of ties, there is little doubt that in the future South African diplomats are not going to enjoy the grace afforded by the Mandela years.

This likelihood stresses the need to attract the right people to the task. It will also demand a new, cooperative relationship between the foreign service and other areas of government, particularly those concerned with international trade and investment. Indeed, given the centrality of commercial issues to international diplomacy and the growing linkage between foreign and domestic policies, an amalgamation of the diplomatic arms of the DFA and the Department of Trade and Industry is long overdue and is currently under review. Ongoing problems of security and stability on the African continent also highlight the need for the DFA and security forces to work well together – unlike, for example, over the Lesotho peace-enforcement mission in September 1998.

Senior officials acknowledge that the hard choices inherent in a more assertive foreign policy – such as, topically, 'what to do' about Zimbabwe or Angola – demand immediate political action ahead of the completion of this bureaucratic reorganization process. It is also recognized that, given its domestic values and interests, South Africa clearly cannot be all things to all people; nor, given its lack of resources, will it realistically be able to do all things equally. Although this bureaucratic vision requires political back-up, this is an encouraging step forward from the foreign policy confusion of the past five years.

## Conclusion

The ANC was elected, and remains supported, by the bulk of South Africans, the majority of whom are black and of the poorer classes. Given this background and also the high expectations that accompanied its accession to power, it remains sensitive to remarks about its lack of socio-economic delivery, so necessary in the fields of housing, electrification, education, policing and, most critically, employment creation. Indeed, there has been a tendency by the party to equate, perhaps quite deliberately, criticism of (a lack of) government delivery with condemnation of the liberation struggle. This attitude perpetuates the morality play that defined South Africa's political landscape during the apartheid period.

All this may appear strange given that the ANC enjoys and will probably retain a nearly two-thirds parliamentary majority. But it reflects the extent of the diverse forces and debate within the broad coalition that makes up the ANC. More especially, it highlights Thabo Mbeki's own preoccupation with his domestic power-base and the seriousness, even sensitivity, with which he views commentary on his leadership and policies.

As South Africa increasingly – albeit slowly – becomes just another country, it will be essential for its politicians and diplomats alike to emphasize its unique role in the global and, especially, regional community. It will also have to play to the strengths of its domestic set-up – the non-belligerent and healthy nature of its democracy, a highly developed financial and economic infrastructure, and a favourable and secure policy environment.

## B: FROM MANDELA TO MBEKI

### David Simon

## The record to date

### The 1994 general election

The 1999 general election will be a very different phenomenon from its 1994 predecessor. On that occasion, the entire future of South Africa was, quite literally, at stake. The traumatic, problem-laden but ultimately predominantly peaceful process of multiparty constitutional negotiation had run its course, and the interim constitution was in place for a non-racial post-apartheid order. The election represented the penultimate act in the process of constitutional transition, to be followed by the swearing in of the new government. Although the ANC was widely expected to win a majority, this could not be taken for granted, and all manner of speculation was rife about possible alliances if matters were finely balanced. Both because of the immense prize at stake and because this was the first genuinely non-racial election in the country's history, nobody was entirely clear about how the black majority would vote. Most of these were first-time voters in national politics; besides, the high levels of intimidation in several areas and of politically inspired violence in KwaZulu-Natal would quite possibly have a marked impact. Also of particular interest – and importance – especially in the Western Cape, was how the minority coloured and Asian communities would vote.

The results were probably about as good as possible for the country as a whole – were there any clearly identifiable 'national interest'. The ANC held a substantial working majority, but one which fell slightly short of the two-thirds required for an effective monopoly on power. However, in terms of the interim constitution, a Government of National Unity was established, with cabinet seats allocated proportionately among parties gaining more than ten per cent of the vote, namely the ANC, Inkatha Freedom Party and the National Party. Seven of the nine new provinces were also under ANC control; the exceptions being KwaZulu-Natal, where the IFP won, and the Western Cape, where the NP emerged victorious as a result of the overwhelming support for it by coloured voters. Under President Nelson Mandela's leadership, the emphasis fell very much on national reconciliation, with consultative mechanisms and the principle of cooperative government between national, provincial and local levels of the state. Perhaps Mandela was taking the cue from neighbouring Namibia, where President Sam Nujoma made this his personal policy at independence in 1990, against the wishes of SWAPO radicals, who felt that this precluded the more substantive redistribution of resources for which they had fought.

## Key changes 1994–9

Over the last five years, the country has changed immeasurably. Inevitably, however, the initial honeymoon enjoyed by the ANC, and especially the almost saintlike status bestowed on President Mandela, has given way to growing cynicism among both black and white South Africans – albeit for different reasons. In terms of political developments, as Stanley Uys and David Welsh point out in different ways, tensions exist within the ANC, which still regards itself as a liberation movement rather than a political party. In particular, many radicals (whether regarding themselves as socialists or not), and even some moderates, are becoming impatient at the slow rate of progress with redistributive policies.

Conversely, the majority of whites, while readily admitting to admiration for Mandela himself, had deluded themselves into thinking that the interim constitution and a non-racial election would guarantee them unchanged lifestyles. Disagreements over style and some policies as well as the final constitution led to the NP's withdrawal from the GNU midway through its term of office. This deprived it of one of the principal levers it had held, and its ability to represent conservative white interests declined substantially. The party has been riven by internal turmoil ever since, and support has diminished markedly. F.W. de Klerk's successor as leader, Marthinus van Schalkwyk, lacks stature, experience and visibility, while the party is widely perceived as increasingly irrelevant. Some whites have also been attracted to the United Democratic Movement (UDM), formed by the disaffected former NP chief constitutional negotiator and cabinet minister, Roelf Meyer, and Bantu Holomisa, erstwhile Transkei strongman and then ANC deputy minister. Although it is intended to appeal to a diverse electorate, the UDM's real support appears modest. Heather Deegan's contribution in Chapter 5 provides insights into recent opinion polls as indicators of party political support.

## Major problem areas

The very real inability of the police to contain the high level of crime, which, following the political transition, became far more visible and violent in former white suburbs, has contributed much to white anger and cynicism. Crime is the number one topic of conversation in white social gatherings, closely followed by allegedly rampant corruption. In fact, there have been some welcome signs that anti-crime campaigns and improved policing and intelligence gathering may be bearing fruit. Recent statistics have also shown that many categories of violent crime – with the signal exception of reported rapes – are now falling in all provinces except the Western Cape. Moreover, whites do not have a monopoly when it comes to being victims of crime: it is still many times more dangerous to live in former black townships than in more exclusive suburbs. However, potential foreign investors do regard the high crime rate as a deterrent, especially when prominent foreign businessmen become victims – as occurred most recently with the murder of the head of Daewoo Motor Corp. in Johannesburg in early February 1999.

It is very difficult to verify claims that corruption is far more widespread than previously. Successive apartheid governments and their policies of fragmentation and creating despotic fiefdoms bred rampant corruption; the entire Department of Development Administration was abolished in the early 1990s for this reason. By contrast, allegations of corruption are far more likely to be aired publicly and to be investigated nowadays. The current raft of investigations and trials relating to senior Mpumalanga officials and cabinet members – right up to and including the provincial premier Matthew Phosa – is a case in point. Another – rather racist – myth is that the alleged rise in corruption is almost entirely due to the Africanization of the civil service. Actually, it also appears increasingly evident in various levels of the private sector where, despite affirmative action (usually styled 'empowerment'), whites still dominate the upper ranks.[1] Corruption is not racially based.

As Jesmond Blumenfeld has illustrated in Chapter 4, the country's overall economic performance has been disappointing since 1995/6. Growth projections have not been achieved, major formal-sector retrenchments are continuing, and the ability to meet the RDP and GEAR targets for economic growth, job creation and social redistribution and development is thereby being severely limited.

---

[1] Commercial crime has increased internationally, not just in South.Africa. An interest group, Business Against Crime, was set up to address the problem, while regular press reports highlight individual cases. About 80 per cent of the 29,000 cases under investigation by the police Commercial Branch in 1996 involved fraud, and only 20 per cent theft. Furthermore, the Office for Serious Economic Offences has faced a rising workload over recent years – 33 cases involving R8.5 billion in 1996 alone (L. Camerer, ed., *Costly Crimes: Commercial Crime and Corruption in South Africa*, Institute of Security Studies, Monograph No. 15, Pretoria, 1997).

## The major social and development gains

In evaluating the last five years, it is important to underscore the many very real gains for South Africa as a whole, and for black people in particular. This also helps to put the problems in some context. For example, the last vestiges of statutory apartheid have been abolished; major budgetary reallocations have taken place in education, health and social welfare (especially for infant care and pensions); a complex and judicially arbitrated land restitution and redistribution programme has begun to operate and is gaining momentum; and several million more poor people now have access to potable water and to electricity. In these last two categories, the ambitious targets set in the Reconstruction and Development Programme have been achieved.

Deliberate empowerment and affirmative action programmes are also helping to increase the proportion of black people in management positions quite substantially. The military budget has been cut by over a quarter as a direct peace dividend, and Merle Lipton's contribution in Chapter 5 has shown how the Truth and Reconciliation Commission has served as something of a national catharsis in the cause of reconciliation, despite its limitations, the controversies it has generated and the criticisms levelled at it from various quarters.

In the international arena, South Africa has enjoyed widespread acclaim. Rehabilitation into the various regional, continental and international institutions, both intergovernmental and non-governmental, was rapid, and expectations have been high all round. South Africa has emerged as a favourite venue for international summits, official and professional conferences and sporting fiestas. The country has been propelled onto the world stage, often in the person of President Mandela, amid expectations of leadership in Africa, participation in international mediation and peacekeeping initiatives, and the like. Yet, as emphasized by Graham Evans, James Barber and James Mayall in Chapter 6, the country has revealed ambivalence and inconsistency in its responses. At one level, Evans and other critics have pointed to an apparently incoherent foreign policy. At another, the government has been at pains to point out that domestic priorities – relating to both post-apartheid reconstruction and the implementation of more appropriate development policies – will take precedence over new international commitments.

Although endeavouring to espouse friendly relations with as many different countries as possible, regardless of political hue, while avoiding causing offence, Mandela has not shied away from controversy in maintaining relations (or repaying political debts) with key solidarity partners of the anti-apartheid era, such as Libya, Cuba and the PLO. Equally, his mediation efforts, even in Africa, have not always proved successful – perhaps most notably in negotiating Mobutu's departure from the former Zaire, and with respect to the Ogoni triallists in Nigeria under Sani Abacha's dictatorship. These arguments are developed in greater detail by Greg Mills.

So, in these contexts, what are the portents for South Africa's second five-year period as a non-racial multiparty democracy?

## The 1999 election and beyond

By contrast with 1994, the 1999 election will be no cliffhanger. The ANC is almost universally regarded as being the certain winner – with Thabo Mbeki therefore set to succeed Mandela as President. The major questions of electoral interest will be:

- whether the ANC gains a two-thirds majority which, under the final constitution now coming into effect, will give it the ability to enact constitutional amendments unilaterally;
- whether the IFP is able to maintain its share of the vote, overwhelmingly concentrated in KwaZulu-Natal and among Zulu migrants in Gauteng;
- whether the New National Party's vote collapses as some observers anticipate, and if so to what extent this reflects shifts by erstwhile white supporters to the far right parties or the traditionally liberal but now increasingly conservative Democratic Party, or by Coloured voters who endorsed the NP in 1994. Certainly, the (N)NP has lost virtually all provincial and local by-elections around the country over the last two years, including in its traditional strongholds, while a number of prominent supporters and officials have recently defected to the DP and two to the ANC;
- whether any new alliance of parties (e.g. the IFP, NNP, DP, UDM) capable of providing a credible opposition emerges ahead of or in the wake of the election;
- whether the ANC is able to gain control of KwaZulu-Natal and/or the Western Cape provincial assemblies.

These issues are important for the complexion of government and the style of governance for millions of South Africans, especially in the two provinces not currently controlled by the ANC. The ANC has emphasized the importance of the two-thirds threshold, perhaps in an effort to rally supporters to vote. In reality, however, it has been able to push through its key legislative programme in the first parliament despite the existence of the GNU and some concessions to gain consensus. In practice, the impact of having a two-thirds majority is therefore likely to be largely symbolic.

The second issue has relevance in terms of relations between the ANC and IFP. These parties appear to be on the verge of forging a pact, although the details are unclear at this stage. If this happens, and it translates into practice, including an end to the violent rivalries on the ground in KwaZulu-Natal, the ANC is likely to be able to gain a two-thirds working majority via this pact; this would offer a kind of insurance policy to the ANC leadership.

This also relates directly to the fourth and fifth issues. As Khehla Shubane has indicated in Chapter 5, there are prospects of different inter-party alliances in different provinces, based on local perceptions of pragmatic self-interest. However, under the party list system of proportional representation under which these elections are to be contested, electoral alliances cannot include decisions not to stand against one another's candidates; therefore agreements are necessarily limited to post-election cooperation. It is far from clear whether any pacts would translate into significant changes in voter behaviour. At present, there does not appear to be any real prospect of a meaningful pact or alliance other than that between the ANC and IFP. Nevertheless, the latter eventuality would, in effect, secure control of KwaZulu-Natal for the ANC-in-alliance, as there is no third party with a chance of gaining power there. On the other hand, there must be doubt over whether an alliance forged at the level of national and provincial leaders would be respected by the grassroots membership of the respective parties. It could easily be ignored or violated, with continued violence undermining it yet further. The murder of Sifiso Nkabinde, the notorious UDM and former ANC warlord, in Richmond at the end of January 1999, and the retribution killings which followed, illustrate the dangers. By contrast with the KwaZulu case, the NP and DP may cooperate to keep the ANC out of power in the Western Cape.

In practice, the larger the ANC's working majority in parliament and the less effective the opposition, the more likely it is to become inward-looking, more auto-cratic and less transparent and accountable. Thabo Mbeki's political persona remains something of an enigma, as several contributions to this study point out. While congenial, widely experienced and diplomatic in his international dealings, he is felt by many to have a more autocratic side. He has certainly shown himself sensitive to public criticism, attacking the media rather gratuitously on several recent occasions, and in a manner which has worried many whites and other liberals, as well as foreign observers. It is difficult to judge at this juncture whether such outbursts reflect his real inclinations, the current political brittleness, or the efforts of some-one without a wide political base within the ANC to garner support from the radical grassroots by threatening the bastions of entrenched power.

## The ANC's trajectory

Beyond the election, the overall direction of ANC policies is unlikely to change dramatically, although the party leadership will seek to entrench its control, quite possibly becoming less tolerant of dissent or even the expression of diverse opinions by its MPs in the national and provincial assemblies. If the ANC gains control of KwaZulu-Natal and/or the Western Cape, policies there will be brought far more in line with overall national policy, something which is expected to speed up policy implementation by reducing the time-consuming and unproductive struggles which have characterized provincial relations with Pretoria. More generally, power struggles, and efforts to reconcile the distribution of powers, responsibilities and resources between central, provincial and local governments, are certain to continue, as the process remains incomplete, the provisions of the final constitution will need to be complied with, and there will remain wide disparities in resourcing and skilled personnel among the provinces and local authorities.

In other spheres, a large parliamentary majority is likely to be reflected in efforts to accelerate various aspects of empowerment and resource redistribution, especially in terms of land, house construction, job opportunities and access to education and health. The current anti-crime initiatives will necessarily continue, but whether the political will to tackle corruption in both public and private sectors will exist remains an open question. On one hand, it would be an effective method for Mbeki to gain the confidence of minority groups and the middle classes, segments of large capital, and foreign donors and investors. On the other, it might alienate radical black elements, who see little wrong with resource redistribution by such means. One other trend which is very likely to increase is 'careerism', as Mandela rather loosely labelled it, or the loss of social conscience and a tendency for people – perhaps most conspicuously within ANC ranks but among blacks generally – to put personal gain and profit above all else. This is not unrelated to my earlier points regarding crime and corruption. One other possibility which cannot be discounted, particularly in view of the probable lack of a strong parliamentary opposition and the likelihood of sharp internal divisions over the above set of issues, is that of a split within the ANC.

## The international arena

Abroad, the government will seek to build on its high international standing, although Mbeki and his Minister of Foreign Affairs will have to work far harder to secure a profile approaching that of Mandela. On the other hand, the latter's increasingly frequent lack of consultation prior to interventions will not be missed. Alfred Nzo, the incumbent minister, is not highly regarded and is unlikely to be representing the country in this capacity after the election; the choice of his successor will be important. Hard work and careful diplomacy will be needed in the southern African subcontinent to repair relations with Zimbabwe and to seek a new consensus for conflict resolution and collaborative development in the wake of the damage done by the current crisis in and over the Democratic Republic of Congo. Whether the Southern African Development Community, seen as the principal regional development institution until deep divisions among its members emerged over the Congo conflict, can regain its momentum remains to be seen. On a continental scale, South Africa will increasingly be sought out as mediator, peace-keeper and spokesperson in negotiations over global trade policy, broader conflicts and environmental concerns. Globally, involvement in fora such as the IOR initiative, the Non-Aligned Movement, the Commonwealth and even the UN will be maintained and enhanced. However, careful balancing of such external engagements and commitments with domestic policy priorities will be needed.

## Outlook

Overall, the second parliament of post-apartheid South Africa is likely to be characterized by a different managerial style, clear efforts by the ANC to consolidate its power, and a reduced tolerance of dissent or diverse opinion. This will cause some concerns in relation to political debate, media freedom and the like. Efforts to accelerate resource distribution will have mixed results, almost certainly still failing to assuage the very high expectations of many black people while raising anxiety in white and other minority communities even further. The police may succeed in checking and reducing the unacceptably high crime levels, something that would raise domestic confidence and enhance prospects for new foreign direct investment. In most respects, however, little radical change in policy orientation or content is likely unless there is a major split within the ANC.